How to Be Happy Though Married

TIM LAHAYE

TYNDALE HOUSE PUBLISHERS, INC., WHEATON, ILLINOIS

Library of Congress Cataloging-in-Publication Data

LaHaye, Tim F.
    How to be happy though married / Tim LaHaye.–rev. and expanded ed.
        p. cm.
    Includes bibliographical references.
    ISBN 0-8423-4352-0 (pbk.)
    1. Marriage—Religious aspects—Christianity.   I. Title.
BV835 .L26 2002
248.8′44—dc21   2002003836

Printed in the United States of America

07   06   05   04   03   02
6   5   4   3   2   1

This book is lovingly dedicated to my wife, Beverly.
Her patient understanding and loving tenderness have made
our marriage an increasingly joyous experience. Her inner beauty,
"the hidden woman of the heart," has improved with the passage
of our more than fifty years together. Every day I thank
God for bringing her into my life.

ACKNOWLEDGMENTS

To my friend and fellow writer, Mike Yorkey. Without his help, due to my overloaded writing schedule with the Left Behind series of fiction books, the Tim LaHaye Prophecy Study Bible, *and several other books on prophecy, this book could not have been completed. I thank God for Mike.*

And to Greg Johnson of Alive Communications for keeping after me until we finished this revised update of what has turned out to be a classic. It is my prayer that, like the original version, How to Be Happy Though Married *will help transform the lives of many who seek a richer and fuller marriage.*

TABLE OF CONTENTS

INTRODUCTION

HOW TO BE HAPPY THOUGH MARRIED was the second book I wrote, way back in 1968, for Tyndale House Publishers in Wheaton, Illinois. A year earlier, Tyndale House had published my first book, *Spirit-Controlled Temperament*, in which I discussed the four basic temperaments of people—their strengths and their weaknesses. When this literary effort took off, Bob Hawkins of Tyndale House asked me to write a book on marriage.

I knew something about marriage because I was known as "Marrying Sam" in San Diego, where I was pastoring Scott Memorial Baptist Church at the time. I usually performed three marriage ceremonies every weekend during the "high season" months of May, June, July, and August. I required young couples to meet with me for premarital counseling before I would marry them, and I invariably ended up seeing more than a few of them *after* the wedding ceremony when life didn't turn out to be a trip down the yellow brick road.

Based upon those counseling experiences, I went to work on *How to Be Happy Though Married*. After completing the manuscript, I mailed two typed copies to Tyndale House (no computers in those days!), where one wound up on the dining-room table of Dr. Ken Taylor, the founder of Tyndale House and the man responsible for writing *Living Letters* and *The Living Bible*.

Dr. Taylor liked the manuscript except for one glaring problem: my chapter on the physical adjustment in marriage. It was too . . . too . . . *frank,* was the word I received from one of Dr. Taylor's associates. Yes, that chapter was all about sex, and as you will see in this revised edition, it contains drawings of the male and female genitalia and detailed descriptions on how to make love.

"Our staff really likes your manuscript," explained Bob Hawkins, "but Dr. Taylor is not sure that Tyndale House wants to be associated with such an overt chapter on sex in a Christian book. We are not convinced that it's appropriate."

I lobbied to include the chapter on physical adjustment, stating that this chapter was needed by the Christian community (Christians make love too, don't they?) and that it would prove helpful. Thankfully, Dr. Taylor came around and *How to Be Happy Though Married* was published just as I had written it. The book remained in print without any revisions, lo these many decades, until Tyndale and I recently agreed that the book needed to be brought into the twenty-first century.

As I set myself to complete that task, I fingered one of the first editions of the book, which contained a color photo of my wife, Bev, and me on the back cover. *Who is that dashing fellow with the jet-black hair?* Well, that was me back then, and while I've changed with the years, the principles contained in this book have not. What *has* changed is how marriage is on the wane in today's society. Couples are cohabiting in breathtaking numbers these days: The number of unmarried couples living together has increased in the past forty years more than tenfold—from about 400,000 to more than 4 million.

Sociologists say the trend reflects a growing disregard for marriage and an acceptance of nontraditional lifestyles. "Marriage is losing much of its status and authority as a social institution," declares the annual report of the National Marriage Project, a nonpartisan initiative aimed at promoting the stability of marriage. This is a shame because God designed men and women to complement each other so that they might each give to the other what each one lacked. This "complementing" best occurs when both sides are *totally* committed to a lifelong relationship, which is what marriage is all about. But these differences that can complement and blend two unique individuals into one can also be incompatibilities that divide and cause separation.

Having said that, marriage can be the most happy, the most mediocre, or the most unhappy of life's experiences. Which is it going to be for you? The daily parts and pieces of marriage do not automatically fall into place with the romantic glamour found in Harlequin novels. Loving and living with your partner takes daily determination and practice—and the giving of oneself for the good of the other.

Since God created man and woman for each other, it follows that the best advice on marriage is in the Bible. God planned marriage for man's good: "And the Lord God said, 'It is not good for the man to be alone. I will make a companion who will help him'" (Genesis 2:18). Later in the second chapter of Genesis it says, "This explains why a man leaves his father and mother and is joined to his wife, and the two are united into one" (verse 24).

Man was the only creature God created alone in the Garden; all the animals were made male and female and had mates. However, human beings were created in the image of God (Genesis 1:26) and given an eternal soul (Genesis 2:7 KJV), and a mere mate was not sufficient for man's emotional and spiritual needs.

Thus, God planned for a man and a woman to be more than mates—to be *helpmates*. Herein lies the secret of a happy marriage. If all two people have in common is the "mating urge," theirs will always be an inadequate relationship scarcely more satisfying than the relationship of animals. In order for couples to find ultimate happiness in marriage, they must work together to make their mental, spiritual, emotional, and physical differences blend into a harmonious relationship.

A man and woman begin their marriage very much in love. Because of their natural sexual and temperamental differences, which gradually become more and more apparent, conflict comes into their relationship. If they don't learn how to resolve conflict, their love will be replaced by hostility and animosity, reducing their chances for a happy marriage.

God wants the home to be a haven of love where husband, wife, and children live with a sense of security and a feeling of acceptance. With all the school shootings and societal violence outside the home, everyone needs a place in life where they are surrounded by peace and love. God ordained the home as that place of emotional safety. Everyone who marries wants that kind of home, but a happy home doesn't just happen. It is the result of two things: proper adjustment to each other and incorporating into daily life the principles of marriage outlined by God in the Bible.

The principles in the following pages are the culmination of my research and counseling with thousands of couples before and after marriage. One thing I can state is that *it's never too late to repair a marriage.* In closing, my prayer is that God will use this revised version of *How to Be Happy Though Married* to help couples adjust to each other and fill their homes with love, warmth, and understanding.

OPPOSITES 1 ATTRACT

ONE OF THE MOST ENDEARING French fairy tales of all time—
Beauty and the Beast—has spawned Broadway musicals, a TV
series, an animated Disney film, board games, a Nintendo action
thriller, ice shows, and thousands of Web sites, all celebrating the
proposition that opposites can and do attract. These days, the
phrase is even employed as shorthand to convey a certain meaning; for example, when Dennis Rodman and Carmen Electra got
married, we knew exactly what the entertainment media meant
when they called the union a "beauty and the beast" marriage.

In its original form, *Beauty and the Beast* is the story of two
people who couldn't be more opposite—Vincent and Katherine.
Vincent is a ferocious, disagreeable character who meets the good-
hearted, virginal Katherine. She sees beneath his contemptible
appearance and gruff mannerisms and falls in love with the furry
creature, warts and all. He falls in love as well, but the Beast is sure
his love can never be requited because of his ugly appearance.
When Katherine trusts her heart and accepts him unconditionally,
Vincent is transformed into a smooth-shaven, handsome young
man, and they live happily ever after.

If only life imitated art. In counseling couples over the last five decades, I've come across numerous "beauty and the beast" personality conflicts that top the list of marital discord.

"Why did I get married in the first place?" is the typical refrain I hear from one of the partners. "We have a hopeless personality conflict! If I say my dress is black, he disagrees and says it's navy blue. We argue about what time it is. We can't even agree on what restaurant serves the best Italian food."

Why do couples bring out the worst in each other? Why do opposite personalities attract each other? Why do two people who are so different get married?

To answer these questions, we need to become acquainted with what makes people tick. Many suggestions have been offered: economic background, length of education, the neighborhood we grew up in, and our ethnic heritage. These characteristics have a bearing on our differences, but so does our temperament—something we inherited in our family genes—and we really don't have much say-so in the matter.

You can find many different theories of personality types in mall bookstores. For the purposes of this discussion, I would like to refer to my book *Spirit-Controlled Temperament,* in which I outlined four basic temperaments and detailed the strengths and weaknesses of these temperaments. My purpose was to show that the Holy Spirit working in the lives of Christians can help them overcome their weaknesses. Allow me to present a condensed description of the four temperaments to show why opposites attract each other.

First of all, human temperament is a fascinating study! Temperament includes the combination of inborn traits that subconsciously affect a person's behavior. These traits, passed on by the genes, include intelligence, race, sex, and many other factors. The alignment of temperament traits stems from four basic types. Many of us are a mixture of temperaments, representing characteristics passed along by parents and grandparents. One temperament type usually dominates in individuals, but strains of one or two others will always be found. For instance, extroverts are predominantly sanguine or choleric in temperament, while introverts are predominantly melancholy or phlegmatic.

Before we dive further into understanding these temperaments, let me state that I know words such as *sanguine* and *choleric* aren't used much in today's language. They are time-honored descriptions of temperament, however, and if you will stick with me and learn them, you will discover a great deal about yourself and your partner. Temperament is an important facet of marital happiness because it helps explain why people with differing personalities are attracted to each other.

One more point: It would be much simpler to report that only four temperaments exist. While I agree that one of the four dominates in each individual's personality, we all have a secondary temperament that to some extent influences our behavior. For instance, my temperament is choleric-sanguine, while Bev is more phlegmatic-sanguine. Keep that point in mind as you read more about the four temperaments.

THE SANGUINE TEMPERAMENT

Men and women with the sanguine temperament are warm, buoyant, and lively. They are naturally receptive, and external impressions easily find their way to their hearts. Their emotions—rather than reflective thoughts—are the basis of most of their decisions.

Sanguine types enjoy people, shy away from solitude, and are at their best when surrounded by friends, where they can take center stage. They have an endless repertoire of interesting stories to tell, making them fun to be around at parties or social gatherings.

Mr. or Mrs. Sanguine is never at a loss for words. Sanguines often speak before thinking, but their open sincerity has a disarming effect on their listeners. Their freewheeling, extroverted ways of living make them the envy of more timid temperament types.

Their noisy, blustering, and friendly demeanor makes them appear more confident than they really are, but their energy and lovable disposition get them through the rough spots of life. People have a way of excusing their weaknesses by saying, "That's just the way Sam is," or "Lisa's always running behind, but you can still count on her."

Cheerful, fun-to-be-around sanguine people enrich the world. They make good salespeople, hospital workers, teachers, flight attendants, news anchors, actors, actresses, public speakers, and community leaders.

Back when they were in high school, the sanguine types were voted "Most Likely to Succeed," but they often fall short of this prediction because of weak wills. Sanguines who find themselves ineffective and undependable tend to become restless, undisciplined, egocentric, and emotionally explosive.

THE CHOLERIC TEMPERAMENT

The choleric temperament is found in people who are hot, quick, active, practical, and strong-willed. They tend to be self-sufficient, independent, decisive, and opinionated, finding it easy to make decisions for themselves as well as for others.

Mr. or Mrs. Choleric thrives on activities. Cholerics love to be involved—not because they seek stimulation but rather because they want to stimulate others with their endless ideas. Their ambitious minds are always "on," planning long-range projects and making snap decisions. They do not vacillate under pressure of what others think. They take definite stands on issues and can often be found crusading for great social causes according to their political bents.

Adversaries seldom frighten them; conversely, cholerics welcome the challenge because they want to prove they are right. They possess dogged determination and often succeed where others fail—not because their plans are better than anyone else's but because they push long after others have become discouraged and quit. These natural-born leaders will storm the hill or take on city hall. Their motto: *Either lead, follow, or get out of the way.*

The cholerics' emotional nature is the least developed part of their temperament. They do not suffer fools gladly, nor do they sympathize easily with others. Male cholerics are often embarrassed or disgusted by the sight of other men crying. They have little appreciation for the fine arts because their primary interests lie in the utilitarian values of life.

They are quick to recognize opportunities and equally as quick at diagnosing the best way to make use of them. Although cholerics are generally well-organized, details bore them. They are not given to contemplation; they prefer making quick, intuitive appraisals. Once they have defined a path, they will run roughshod over individuals who stand in their way, although these opportunists have a Machiavellian streak that is not above sneaky end arounds.

Many of the world's great generals and leaders have been cholerics. They make good executives, idea men, producers, dictators, or criminals, depending on their moral standards. They can be no-nonsense department heads, cops, or Sunday school directors. I remember a Vacation Bible School director our church had one time. That summer, our VBS program was the best-run one ever, but the following year, we couldn't get any workers because the director had been so rude to everybody.

Cholerics, male or female, have a hard time with people skills. They don't need babying or pampering, and it's hard for them to adapt their styles to the needs of other people. Cholerics are difficult folks to live with. They can come across as hot-tempered, cruel, impetuous, and self-sufficient. The person with this temperament is often more appreciated by friends and associates than by members of his or her family.

THE MELANCHOLY TEMPERAMENT

Melancholy people are often dark, moody individuals prone to analyzing everything to death. Nonetheless, they can be self-sacrificing, gifted perfectionists with sensitive emotional natures. No one appreciates strolling the great halls of the Louvre Museum more than melancholic people do. That's why many of the world's great artists, musicians, inventors, philosophers, and educators have been of the melancholy temperament.

These self-described introverts come hardwired with a variety of moods dominated by their emotions. Sometimes melancholics' moods will lift them to heights of ecstasy ("I just loved the new Julia Roberts movie!"), but five minutes later, they can become gloomy and depressed ("I just can't seem to snap out of it"). If this occurs, spouses need to watch out. Withdrawn melancholics can be quite antagonistic and hard on a marriage.

When they're in a good mood, melancholics are your best buddies and friends. Unlike sanguine men and women, however, they do not make friends easily. Melancholics are initially reserved when meeting people, preferring for new acquaintances to come to them. They are perhaps the most dependable of all the temperaments because their perfectionist tendencies do not permit them to let others down. Their natural reluctance to remain in the background is not an indication that they don't like people but that they are simply reluctant to take people at face value. Thus, they have their guards up and act suspiciously when others shower them with attention.

Melancholics have an uncanny ability to figure out what to do when obstacles are placed in their paths. If a project needs to be completed within a seemingly impossible time frame, you can be sure a melancholic will find a way. This foresight contrasts sharply with cholerics, who rarely anticipate problems but are confident they can handle anything that comes their way.

Mr. or Mrs. Melancholy usually finds the greatest meaning in life through personal sacrifice. Melancholics are quite willing to put aside their personal desires if the sacrifice is worth it and accomplishes something for the greater good. This turns their cranks, as they say. Finally, melancholy people have much natural potential when energized by the Holy Spirit.

THE PHLEGMATIC TEMPERAMENT

Everyone loves to be around those with phlegmatic temperaments. They act calm, cool, and collected. They travel through life in the slow lane, content to take it easy. Life for phlegmatic people is one happy, pleasant experience after another, which is why they avoid entanglements with others as much as possible.

Phlegmatic types seldom get ruffled. They are the types who rarely express anger or laugh until tears are running down their cheeks. Their temperament remains steady, like Old Man River. Beneath their cool, reticent, almost timid personalities, phlegmatics draw from a good combination of abilities. They feel more emotion than appears on the surface and have a great capacity to appreciate the fine arts and the better things of life.

Since phlegmatics enjoy people, they do not lack for friends. They are natural-born raconteurs who love to hear a good story as much as they enjoy telling one. Known for their dry sense of humor, they have the ability to see the lighter side in everyday situations. Their retentive minds delight in poking fun at the other temperament types. Annoyed by the aimless, restless enthusiasm of sanguine people, they often confront sanguines with the futility of such enthusiasm ("Sorry, Charlie, but it's not going to work"). They are disgusted by the gloomy moods of melancholy folks and have been known to ridicule them ("Get a life"). They can even throw ice water on the bubbling plans of cholerics ("Fuggettaboutit").

Phlegmatics make great armchair quarterbacks, preferring to be spectators in life and keep others at arm's length. They like routine; anyone trying to get them to step out of their comfort zone will be met with reluctance. This does not mean, however, that phlegmatics cannot appreciate the need for action or empathize with the difficulties of others.

For instance, cholerics view social injustice with a crusading spirit, causing them to say, "Let's get a committee organized and do something about this!" A phlegmatic would be more likely to respond by saying, "These conditions are terrible! Why doesn't someone do something about them?" Phlegmatics are often kind-hearted and sympathetic, which is why the world has greatly benefited from their gracious nature. They make excellent diplomats, office managers, accountants, elementary-school teachers, scientists, account reps, or other meticulous, detail-oriented workers.

The chief weakness of phlegmatics, which often keeps them from fulfilling their potential, is their dearth of motivation. Some husbands will say this about their phlegmatic wives: "She is a wonderful wife and mother, but she is one lousy housekeeper." A frustrated wife might say, "Joe is a wonderful husband, but he can't seem to get a promotion." Although they are easy to live with, phlegmatics have a careless, low-pressure way of living that can irritate a hyperactive partner to no end.

Phlegmatics make good companions to their children because they find it easy to stop what they are doing and play with the children.

WHY OPPOSITES ATTRACT

The subconscious mind has far more influence on us than most people realize. This is graphically seen in the way we select our friends—and particularly in our choice of a life partner. Loud, gregarious, and extroverted sanguines subconsciously wish they could control themselves better. When they return from a party, the realization that they chattered endlessly and tended to dominate conversations often, in retrospect, embarrasses them.

Sweet, quiet phlegmatics or melancholics subconsciously think, *I wish I could be more outgoing and expressive.* It is very easy to see why these contrasting types will be interested in each other when they meet. He is everything she wishes to be, and she is just what he would secretly like to be; thus, they seem to complement each other. This principle is subconsciously at work every time a person singles out the one he or she desires to marry. In fact, no temperament is subconsciously barred to a person but his or her own. The important thing to note is that people are attracted to each other on the basis of strengths, but each natural strength has a corresponding weakness.

WEAKNESSES APPEAR LATER

Most couples are so head over heels in love that they see only the *good parts* of their fiancé or fiancée. It doesn't take much time after the honeymoon—a few days, a few weeks—before the novelty of being married wears off and each partner's flaws become known. Every human being comes fully equipped with a bucketful of weaknesses, though this news may come as a shock to naïve newlyweds. These weaknesses call for adjustments to be made in the relationship. Not only that, young couples will have to learn to *live* with their partner's weaknesses.

That's why it's so important for married couples to have the Holy Spirit's help so that they might be *gentle, patient, kind, and self-controlled* while adjusting to this new calculus. Fortunately for us, the Holy Spirit helps turn weaknesses into positive attributes. Galatians 5:22-23 points out nine characteristics available for Spirit-filled Christians: love, joy, peace, patience, kindness, goodness, faithfulness, gentleness, and self-control. That's quite a laundry list.

Spirit-filled Christians attain more enjoyment in their marriage because they seek the Holy Spirit's help to overcome their weaknesses, which helps them become less objectionable to their partner. In addition, the Holy Spirit gives them grace to overlook and joyously live with their partner's weaknesses.

Personality Conflicts

Personality conflicts are, in reality, differing weaknesses that could be called *temperament conflicts.* They are weaknesses in one partner that irritate the weaknesses in the other. Here are some examples I have encountered in counseling.

Mr. Sanguine's carelessness and unfinished projects create a great conflict with his wife's melancholy, perfectionist, and faithful tendencies. When he comes home from a sales meeting at

8:00 P.M., hours after his wife's home-baked lasagna came out of the oven at 5:45 P.M., she will have a hard time "forgiving and forgetting" his thoughtlessness, because he didn't even pick up his cell phone to say he'd be late. Mr. Choleric devotes his active mind to the business of making a living, and his wife feels neglected. She doesn't realize that before marriage she was his "project" and that he pursued and pursued until she agreed to marry him. Now that he can cross off "get married" from his to-do list, he rushes off to the next step in his master plan, which is to buy their first house and move out of their dumpy apartment. He works long hours to get ahead and make more money, but when he comes home, all he can do is express irritation at their messy surroundings. Instead, he should realize that his wife is employed outside the home as well and is often too tired to keep the apartment neat as a pin. His cruel, sarcastic words feel like a lash against her back.

Now let's take a look at Mrs. Melancholy, who seems to have permanent PMS—at least that is what her new husband thinks. She's been in a black mood ever since the jet landed at home following the Hawaiian honeymoon. Perhaps she experienced a natural letdown after the tense, excited anticipation of her wedding, but she is not sure. All she knows is her husband seems impatient and frustrated with her, which causes the young bride to lapse into periods of silence and crying jags. *He doesn't love me anymore,* she thinks. She focuses her perfectionist tendencies on creating a flawlessly kept house, but that turns out to be counterproductive when her husband feels as though he can't relax in his own home. She chides him for putting his bare feet on the coffee table or for not tossing his socks into the clothes hamper. Her mounting frustrations stay bottled up, where they will ultimately explode and cause a major argument.

Mrs. Phlegmatic's lack of motivation becomes a drain on her husband. Although she has an exciting career as a buyer for a department store chain, she prefers to cocoon at home when not at the office. Her husband feels as if he's married the most boring person on earth. He begs and pleads for her to do something with him—like take out their mountain bikes for a ride. He says to himself, *It's just so hard for her to get going on a Saturday morning.* Her quiet stubbornness has created great resentment and frustration in her husband's heart.

Manage Your Conflicts

Differences between partners need not be fatal! No disagreement is a threat to a marriage; it's what a couple does about those disagreements that determines the success or failure of a marriage. The following suggestions are given to help you make the right kind of adjustments.

* **When you feel frustration, resentment, or some other form of hostility, stop and take an objective look at what's causing it.**
* **Pray about it.** Ask God to give you a peace that does not depend upon your partner's behavior. After facing your inner hostility and realizing that anger is a sin, confess it (1 John 1:9) and ask God to fill you with his Spirit (Luke 11:13). Then you will be able to walk in the Spirit (Galatians 5:16, NKJV).
* **Next, pray about your partner's actions, asking God to help your spouse see his or her shortcomings and to lead you in discussing the matter with him.**
* **Communicate with your partner about what you perceive as his or her faults. This should always be done** *in love* (Ephesians 4:15). Pick a relaxed time when you can objectively

share your feelings without getting overly emotional. This is usually best accomplished when you go out to dinner. Never raise your voice in anger, and always allow time for her to think about what you've said. Then leave the matter up to the Holy Spirit.

* **Ask God, the giver of love, to fill you with so much love for your spouse that you can genuinely love your partner despite his or her weaknesses.** Look at his strengths and thank God for them (1 Thessalonians 5:18).

* **Forget past mistakes!** "Forgetting the past and looking forward to what lies ahead, I strain to reach the end of the race and receive the prize for which God, through Christ Jesus, is calling us up to heaven" (Philippians 3:13-14).

If you repeatedly follow this procedure, you will find that the Holy Spirit will lead your reaction to your partner's actions. Your love will increase so much that, like a thick coat of oil-based paint, it will cover a multitude of weaknesses.

FORGET 2 YOURSELF

"WHAT ARE YOUR THOUGHTS ABOUT STARTING A FAMILY?"

I love posing this question during premarital counseling sessions. The young couple often blushes, as if now the whole world knows they will be making love after the nuptials. Then the bride-to-be blurts out, "We don't intend to have children for at least four years! That way we will have time to adjust to each other before we have children."

I nod. That is the most common answer I have received over the years. Her response reflects conventional wisdom: Most couples expect a period of adjustment in their early years of marriage.

How long does this period of adjustment last? From my experience in marriage counseling, I would say around three years. The thirty-six-month mark in marriage is a revealing one; statistics show that seven out of ten divorces occur within the first three years of marriage. Most happily married couples would agree, after looking back through the passage of time, that their first three years contained difficult adjustments that they would prefer not to experience again.

Most marriage counselors acknowledge three basic areas of

marital adjustment: mental, physical, and spiritual. Proper adjustment in each of these areas is necessary to create a well-rounded marriage. If we were to let a circle represent the total marriage, then each of the three adjustment areas would represent about one-third of the total relationship. Although the age of the couple when they married and the length of their marriage are factors that can make one area more important than another, the three areas are approximately equal in importance over a lifetime of marriage. In the twenties, the physical aspects tend to dominate the others, but in the thirties the mental comes to the fore over the physical and spiritual. From the late thirties on, the spiritual usually dominates the others.

These three adjustment areas are always interdependent. It is unusual for couples to have a good physical adjustment if they do not have a high degree of mental adjustment. I have known couples whose difficulty in adjusting mentally produced physical maladjustment, but because of their strong spiritual relationship—a deep, well-grounded faith in Christ—they could improve their mental and physical adjustments. The spiritual is potentially the most important because it can radically improve the adjustment in the other two areas. Because of the great significance of these three adjustment areas, I will deal with them individually in successive chapters, beginning with the mental adjustment area.

For now, let me state that the mental adjustment in marriage, while usually the most complex, offers an exciting opportunity for two people to get to know each other deeply. Since individuals are prone to be on their best behavior throughout courtship, married couples usually have tremendous mental adjustments to make not long after the rice hits the ground. This area of adjustment highlights background differences and encompasses a variety of experiences that require retraining.

In physically adjusting, a couple starts out learning a whole new experience—the beauty of sexual love. In the spiritual realm they can, through the study of the Word of God, similarly learn a new relationship to each other and to God. But in the mental area, each has spent approximately twenty or more years adjusting to other people according to his or her own patterns. Now they come into marriage, with its responsibilities and natural pressures, and they find that their patterns of adjustment to certain experiences conflict with their partner's patterns. Therefore, take special note of the golden rule of mental adjustment as found in Philippians 2:3-4:

> *Don't be selfish; don't live to make a good impression on others. Be humble, thinking of others as better than yourself. Don't think only about your own affairs, but be interested in others, too, and what they are doing.*

With determination before God to forget yourself and make your partner as happy as these verses teach, you cannot help but make wholesome adjustments to the many mental facets of married life. I shall discuss five of the most common problems of mental adjustment.

FINANCES

Financial adjustment is perhaps the most difficult and can place tremendous stresses on a young marriage—usually because there's more month than money to go around. A survey of 125 Christian couples for the book *Saving Money Any Way You Can* revealed that 67 percent said they were struggling to stay ahead or living paycheck to paycheck. The pressure to live within their means, they said, caused dissension and even led to marital breakups.

But who handles the money? The answer to this question is far more significant than just dollars and cents because God has stated very clearly in his Word that the man should be the head of the house. This principle produces happiness; a violation of this principle produces misery. I have never known a happy henpecked husband, nor have I ever met a happy henpecker.

Whether or not he actually writes the bills or balances the checkbook, as the leader of the home, a husband must always be fully aware of how a couple's money is managed. A *team* effort is called for here because they are one flesh. This is why I do not believe in separate bank accounts; both paychecks should be deposited into one family account. This reinforces the idea that you're both rowing in the same boat. Marriage is a joint venture between two people who live as one; it is not two distinct corporations doing business under the same roof.

Likewise, big-ticket purchases (furniture, appliances, and cars, for example) should be made by joint agreement. It's been said that when a woman goes shopping, she comes home with a dress, but when a man goes shopping, he comes home with a powerboat. This can't happen! Anytime one of the partners is opposed to a particular purchase, it would be far better to wait until there is agreement than to defy the other's feelings on the matter.

Where Does It All Go?

Before you can work together, you need to know where your money is going. Christian financial counselors say that very few couples have a budget and actually follow it. That's easy to understand because budgets are a hassle, involve much time to implement, and are no fun. Still, you need to do something. If your financial locomotive is almost out of steam by payday, you must get a handle on your family's living expenses. Today's computer programs like *Quicken* or *Money Manager* make it easy to establish categories for assigning expenses. If you don't have a home computer, then an old spiral notebook will do. Begin by tracking your expenses for three months. Not only will you get a good idea of where you stand, but you'll also have a better sense of where your finances are headed. Then if you get hit with a bigger-than-usual bill—a five-hundred-dollar car repair, for instance—you'll know what areas to cut back.

Start by gathering your receipts, checkbooks, and credit-card statements for the last month or two. Using a software program or your notebook, establish categories that you can assign each expense to. Most young couples have the following monthly expenses:

* rent (or mortgage payments, which must include property tax and house insurance)
* student loans
* groceries
* clothes
* health-insurance premiums
* utilities (electricity, natural gas, heat/air conditioning, water)
* phone
* trash removal
* cable TV and Internet access
* gasoline
* car payments
* car repairs
* car insurance
* newspaper and magazine subscriptions
* haircuts
* charitable giving (church, missionaries)
* restaurants (including McDonald's and take-out pizza)
* vacation
* miscellaneous

Notice that I did not include any expenses for children, which usually come later. After totaling your expenditures, itemize and add up your sources of income:

* husband's take-home pay
* wife's take-home pay
* any moonlighting income

Now take a cold, hard look. How much is the difference between what went out and what came in? Does it look like you're probably spending more than what's coming in? If so, that's not good. The average couple spends about 110 percent of their income, which means they are living beyond their means.

By God's standard, that is not very smart. Proverbs 21:20 tells us, "The wise man saves for the future, but the foolish man spends whatever he gets" (TLB). If you live according to this proverb, you will eliminate 95 percent of your money problems. Interestingly, most folks don't understand that the Bible is the best book on finances ever written. Proverbs is filled with great financial advice, such as: "Good planning and hard work lead to prosperity" (Proverbs 21:5) and "Don't weary yourself trying to get rich. Why waste your time? For riches can disappear as though they had the wings of a bird!" (Proverbs 23:4-5).

Women Working Outside the Home

These days, many young women come into a marriage with budding careers. They may have devoted years of schooling to their field of expertise, or they may have taken a certain job or pursued a certain career path after high school or college. Naturally, many young women continue working after the honeymoon for various reasons: They enjoy the sense of accomplishment and the stimulating work environment, they have the goal of saving enough to make a down payment on a home, or they want to help their husband pursue his career goals or get established in a business. This arrangement should be only until children come into the home, however, which I'll expand upon later in this book.

Be careful that your career doesn't take precedence over children. Listen to this wise advice and follow it closely: If you wait until you can afford to have children, you will probably never have them. Talk to any young parents, and they will tell you the same thing. You can never *afford* children, but you somehow make do, as billions of couples have before you—including your parents! Young couples with children will tell you that children are such a source of enrichment and blessing to them that they couldn't imagine life without those little ones. Don't wait too long to enjoy the blessings of parenthood.

Indebtedness

One of the severe problems in many marriages is that within six months after marriage, couples find themselves hopelessly in debt. This financial strain produces tensions and fears that are an unnecessary hindrance to a proper adjustment.

By debt, I'm talking about credit cards, department-store cards, furniture loans, and other installment debt. I'm afraid that many young couples look at their monthly credit-card statement and say, *This is not a bill. We're not expected to pay in full. We can send in the minimum payment, and everything will be okay.*

Everything won't be okay. Let me make this clear:

You must pay off the credit-card balance in full every month. Otherwise, cut up your cards.

I don't want to sound harsh, but 18 percent interest on your credit-card debt will mortgage your future and escort you rather quickly toward financial ruin. You should not use a credit card unless you can say to yourself, "I could pay for this today—along with everything else that I've charged this month—if I wrote a check." If you know you will not be able to pay off your credit card in its entirety when it's due, then you shouldn't make the purchase. Use a debit card instead, which takes the funds immediately out of your checking account.

This attitude will curb impulse buying. Sure, there is always something to purchase in the early stages of a marriage, but as you'll find out, there's always something to buy no matter how many years you've been married. The wife's attitude toward possessions is very important; she can unconsciously drive her husband to overextend himself in an effort to please her. She should avoid comparisons between the home her father could provide and the little apartment and frugal conditions under which she starts her marriage. Remember that parents have had twenty or thirty years in which to accumulate the possessions they enjoy, and in due time a young couple may hope for the same. The wife's patience and joyous acceptance of her husband's financial capabilities are among the ways she can invest in a long-lasting and happy marriage.

Fiscal Responsibility

In determining how much your lifestyle will cost you, you need to back up and insert two assertions:

1. We will give 10 percent to our church and various charities.
2. We will set aside 10 percent for savings.

As a Christian couple, you can start out immediately securing God's blessing on your family finances according to Malachi 3:3-11 by giving him one-tenth of your income.

If you do not begin your marriage with these two practices, you will find it difficult to start later, but it is not impossible. Give God the tithe and trust him to guide you through your financial problems. He never fails.

Bev and I have always tithed, ever since I made fifteen dollars a week in my first pastorate. I learned this principle from my mother, who made sixty cents an hour working in a factory during the Great Depression years of the 1930s. All I can say is that Matthew 6:33 really works: "But seek first the kingdom of God and His righteousness, and all these things shall be added to you" (NKJV). Tithing doesn't cost you anything. It increases the blessings from God and increases your faith.

Impossible, you say?

You literally can accomplish more financially with God's blessing on the expenditure of 90 percent than you can on the expenditure of 100 percent without God's blessing. I have never known a couple that was not blessed by tithing, which proves the beauty of Scripture to me: "'Bring all the tithes into the storehouse so there will be enough food in my Temple. If you do,' says the Lord Almighty, 'I will open the windows of heaven for you. I will pour out a blessing so great you won't have enough room to take it in! Try it! Let me prove it to you!'" (Malachi 3:10).

Saving the second 10 percent—and really stashing it away in a money-market account or similar investment tool—is what will give you money to draw on when you purchase your "starter" home. My recommendation is that you try to live on the husband's paycheck in the early years of marriage and deposit 100 percent of the wife's paycheck into the bank, where it can earn interest until you've saved enough to make a down payment on your first home or condominium.

With the rest of your money, you can save so you can pay cash for big-ticket items. Don't buy on credit or fall for the "No payments until next year!" pitch. You can avoid expensive interest charges and the pressure of payments by purchasing something only when you have the money in hand.

SOCIAL LIFE AND LEISURE ACTIVITIES

Another significant area of mental adjustment is your social life and leisure activities. God created human beings for fellowship with himself and with one another. Unfortunately, many couples forget that when they marry their spouse, they also inherit a new set of friends.

Leisure activities are also important for you as a couple because they allow you to enjoy common interests together. God wants us to experience the goodness of life and take some time off. God set a great example for us: "On the seventh day, having finished his task, God rested from all his work" (Genesis 2:2). God didn't need to rest after creating the heavens and earth, but he did. You should too. How you socialize and pursue recreation can point out differences between you and your partner—ones that you never dreamed existed. One sports-happy husband and his music-loving wife had this conversation about a year after they were married:

"Why is it that you won't go to UCLA football games with me anymore?" he asked.

"Well, I really don't understand football, so I just don't enjoy it," she replied.

"You've got to be kidding me," he retorted with exasperation. "When we were going out together, you never turned me down when I invited you to go to a Bruins game. I know you were as excited as I was when we beat USC in the Big Game."

Her reply was enlightening. "Oh, I'll tell you why I was excited," she said. "I enjoyed being with you so much I didn't care where we went."

Then it was her turn to ask a question: "Why is it that you don't take me to concerts like you did when we were dating?"

"I can't stand listening to those divas like Whitney Houston!"

That's when the couple realized that in their courtship days their love for each other had anesthetized them to their social differences. The thrill of being together made unpleasant things enjoyable.

This couple worked things out by seeing the wisdom of honoring their differences and pledging to do things together anyway. In principle, this meant that she accompanied him to the Rose Bowl for UCLA football games, and he willingly accompanied her to see some great concerts at Staples Arena. When her taste in music "matured" to include classical music, he even joined her for classical concerts at the Los Angeles Philharmonic. His winning attitude helped her agree to watch those boring baseball games at Chavez Ravine. She even came around to enjoying foot-long Dodger dogs and peanuts and Cracker Jack.

We are all subject to change, and often our likes and dislikes are based purely on bad experiences from the past. Being willing to do for your partner what you would hope your mate would willingly do for you is the foundation of a great marriage.

Friends Are Important

It's fun to do couple-to-couple activities together, which is why we seek the companionship of other married couples. It's also fun to spend time with good friends, even if they are still single. They are part of our life.

Each marriage introduces a new set of friends and associates to the equation, which causes adjustments to be made. Since friends can have a great influence upon us, it is essential that young couples find other Christian friends as close companions, since these friends can help you grow in faith. Yes, you should also have non-Christian friends, who can benefit from a godly influence in their lives—you. Ask the Holy Spirit to help you introduce them to Christ.

The best place to find Christian companionship is in your church. Larger churches often have some sort of a "Young Couples" Sunday school class, which is a great opportunity to learn about married life while meeting other couples similar in age and life experiences to you. Be willing to participate in group outings or open your home to entertaining other couples. Be a friend and make a friend. The old principle, "He that would have friends must show himself friendly," is also true for couples.

THE IN-LAWS

Ever heard this joke?

The doorbell rang. When the young man opened the door, there was his mother-in-law standing on the front step, suitcase in hand.

"Can I stay here for a few days?" she asked in her sweet voice.

"Sure you can," he replied. And then he shut the door in her face.

Okay, so that's a typically rude mother-in-law joke, but getting along with your in-laws is no laughing matter. Your relationship to your spouse's family is important. While every family occasionally experiences major friction, that is an exception rather than the rule. If you haven't encountered in-law troubles, just wait until your first holiday season—especially if both sets of parents live in your region. They will be arguing about who will eat with whom on Thanksgiving and Christmas Day.

Besides divvying up the holiday meals, some parents continue to, well, *parent* their adult children. These parents cannot "cut the apron strings," to use a phrase commonly employed during the era when Bev and I married. Some parents can't resist meddling and throwing in their two cents because "we want the best for you." This drives a wedge between a young couple, even to the point of their rejecting good advice just because it comes from one set of parents.

It's natural for us to think that *our* parents are not as annoying as *our spouse's* parents, simply because we understand our own mother and father better. Many times an in-law's suggestions sound disapproving, when in reality they were given with the best of intentions.

You can afford to be considerate and thoughtful of your partner's parents. After all, they invested many years and thousands of dollars in raising your mate, which means they deserve to be treated with dignity and respect. (Believe us, you'll feel the same way twenty-five or thirty years from now.) Avoid speaking negatively to your partner's parents; if you feel they are interfering too much in your marriage, let your spouse do the talking, although you should accompany him or her if clarification is needed.

The maternal instinct being what it is, mothers frequently have greater difficulty giving up their sons than fathers do giving up their daughters. A loving wife should try to understand this and not put her husband into the difficult position of having to choose his loyalties—his wife or his mother. With thoughtfulness and love, the wife can help her husband maintain a relaxed feeling toward his parents and particularly his mother. This considerateness will also benefit the wife, as calm waters make for a calm marriage.

A husband should be careful to avoid comparisons between his wife and his mother. It is entirely unfair to compare a young wife's cooking skills and housekeeping abilities (or lack thereof) to those of a woman with twenty or more years of experience. Indulging in unkind comparisons of this nature will only create hostilities and conflict between the two women most important to the husband.

Difficulties in family relationships should be talked over carefully and dealt with lovingly. It is possible, with God's help, to have an enjoyable relationship with in-laws that can actually enrich your marriage. And that's no joke!

APPEARANCE

M-Day plus one: In a moment of truth, the young husband discovers what his day-old wife looks like with stringy hair, sleepy eyes, and an unpainted face. While appearance isn't everything, it certainly counts for *something!* The Bible reminds us that "people judge by outward appearance, but the Lord looks at a person's thoughts and intentions" (1 Samuel 16:7). Since your husband is human and a visually driven male, he will look upon your outward appearance. It is therefore important that you do not use a wedding certificate as an excuse to walk around in curlers and gray sweatpants all day.

As for you guys, you never would have been attractive to your wife if you were not clean and neat in appearance. Help keep her love alive by continuing to look well-groomed. This means shaving every day—even if Hollywood thinks the three-day beard is the hippest thing since DVD. Splash some cologne on your neck and face. Wear a stylish haircut. Don't parade around the house in your underwear. Show a little class. Leave the toothpicks in the kitchen and floss in private.

Ladies, we know we don't have to remind you to maintain your beautiful appearance. Your husband feels proud when he introduces you to friends; don't "let yourself go" just because it's just the two of you at home. Wear cute outfits and fun casual clothes, but remember this: if you choose to walk around in your bra and panties, you do so at your own risk!

COURTESY

Courtesy and manners should be part and parcel of every Christian's life, but these social niceties are ignored or even sneered at today. Believe it or not, courtesy is timeless because it's based on the Golden Rule: Do unto others as you would have them do unto you. Good manners never go out of style, no matter how many silly sitcoms you watch on TV.

Unfortunately, courtesy and manners seem to be a dying art. If your husband lacks these qualities, the obvious time to discuss your differences was before the marriage. Now that you have said your "I do"s, what should you do?

When my mother insisted that we always wear a shirt at mealtime, refrain from putting our elbows on the table, say please to one another, and use good manners in our treatment of each other, she remarked, "You will never be in better company than the company you are in right now." I am most grateful for her insistence upon these things because I married a woman who enjoys courtesy and politeness. I am inclined to believe that most women do.

A woman likes to be treated like a lady; therefore, a husband should continue giving his wife "preferential treatment" after they are married. It is a wise husband who opens doors, including car doors, for his wife and generally treats her as a gentleman should treat a lady. You will be making an investment in your wife's happiness and self-respect, which will increase her love for you. Since love begets love, this is one of the best investments you can make in your marriage.

Once, while holding a family conference in an Arizona church, I announced that during the next evening's session I would tell men "how to get your wife to treat you like a king." For some strange reason, we had our largest crowd the next night. "Are you ready to know how to get your wife to treat you like a king?"

"Yes!" I heard hundreds of male voices say.

"Then treat her like a queen!"

My advice startled some of the men for its simplicity, but it works.

DON'T AIR YOUR GRIEVANCES TO OTHERS

One almost inexcusable marital practice is disloyalty. Have you ever been out with a group of friends some night and heard a wife or husband berate and criticize his or her spouse? Partners who cannot communicate in private and seek the safety of the group to vent their pent-up wrath engage in this embarrassing practice. It is one of the most damaging wrongs a person can commit against his or her partner.

Never, *never* air your partner's shortcomings, weaknesses, or deficiencies in front of other people. Never criticize him to your friends or relatives. Never tell demeaning stories about her in public. If you are displeased with your partner's behavior on a matter, there are only two with whom you should share it: God and your partner.

"But I have to tell *someone*," you say.

Phooey. As a Christian, you have someone to whom you can take your problems: your heavenly Father. After a season of prayer and the leading of the Holy Spirit, share the problems with your partner. If this does not work, talk the matter over with your pastor or counselor.

A lovely Christian mother whose daughter married one of the

finest young men in our church came to see me one day. She was troubled over her feelings of animosity and bitterness toward her son-in-law and was finding it increasingly difficult to be nice to him. After talking to her and her daughter one evening, I found the cause.

Two weeks after the couple returned from their honeymoon, they had a fight. The daughter called her mother and told her the whole story. That night the husband came home from work and apologized for his short-tempered treatment of his bride. She accepted his apology, and they had one of those wonderful "making up" experiences that are such a uniting blessing in marriage.

A few weeks later another argument occurred, and the young woman called her mother from the office to pour out her troubled heart, never once mentioning how they had tenderly patched things up before. Without realizing it, the young woman was painting a picture of a one-sided relationship in which the new son-in-law was an "ill-tempered brute" in the mother's eyes. It was only when the daughter disclosed the touching moments of "making up" that she put an end to her mother's resentment.

You should never criticize your partner in front of others for two reasons. First, rehearsing grudges or nursing gripes stamps them more indelibly upon your mind. Second, the desire for approval is one of our basic drives. Nothing can make us feel less approved than to find that our partner has been criticizing us to an outsider. To repeat: If you must talk to someone else, make that person a pastor or a professional counselor. Otherwise, don't discuss the situation with anyone else. And when the children come along, make it a point *never* to criticize your mate in front of them.

BE OPEN TO CHANGE

Most spontaneous decisions or prejudices are the result of our backgrounds, but that does not determine whether they are right or wrong. I have met men who—because their father ignored their mother—refuse to give in to their wife's desire that her husband be more gentlemanly and polite. Actually, that reason has nothing to do with it. Just because a man's father made a lifetime of mistakes is no reason for his son to perpetuate them.

Therefore, whenever you go into a communication session with your partner regarding the mental adjustments of your marriage, always bear in mind that the standards and concepts produced by your background could be wrong. There may be another way of doing things. Remember, one of the characteristics of love is that it "does not demand its own way" (1 Corinthians 13:5).

Adjusting in marriage can be a thrilling experience when enhanced by an effort to improve yourself. Embrace the strengths of your partner's background and temperament. Be willing to bend and give. Don't resist change in your behavior unless it is behavior for which Scripture has already set a standard. Be objective about the differences between you and your partner. Just as you expect her to change in some areas, she has a right to expect changes from you.

Fortunately, change is a natural part of life. Give your partner time to adjust, and you will find that time draws two loving people closer together.

SPIRITUAL 3 ADJUSTMENT

MEN AND WOMEN ARE INTENSELY spiritual creatures. The older
we get, the more conscious we become of this fact. Blaise Pascal,
the seventeenth century French physicist and philosopher, said,
"There is a God-shaped vacuum in the heart of every man which
cannot be satisfied by any created thing, but only by God, the
Creator, who is made known through Jesus Christ." When Jesus
Christ is invited into a person's life as Lord and Savior, this vacuum
is filled. Because of the presence of Jesus Christ, we may have
communion with God—a communion that enriches all areas of
our life.

We talked earlier about how Galatians 5:22-23 describes the
work of God's Spirit in the life of a Christian. As we submit
ourselves to the Holy Spirit, we begin to develop increasing
amounts of love, joy, peace, and patience. Jesus points out the
universal principle that we reap what we sow; therefore, love (or
any other attribute) that is consistently given will be returned to
the giver. It follows then that couples who are giving and receiving
spiritual attributes set themselves down a path toward a delightful
and satisfying marriage.

Men and women cannot make satisfying physical adjustments unless they are first mentally adjusted, but mental adjustments have many complexities. In addition, everyone is vulnerable to selfishness—which hinders mental adjustment—so problems in this area are not easy to solve. That's why I conclude that the spiritual area is the essential component of marital adjustment.

Over the years, I have observed that a good spiritual life will greatly improve mental adjustments. Since the Bible is still the greatest handbook on human behavior, when two people are related to the God of the Bible and to his Word, they will find that his principles will aid them in their spiritual adjustment. Allow me to present five areas of spiritual adjustment that can make your marriage as thrilling and solid as a game-winning Mark McGwire home run in the bottom of the ninth inning.

1. CONSISTENT CHRISTIAN BEHAVIOR

You are the key to the spiritual life of your marriage. Therefore, consistent Christian behavior in the home is a key to spiritual adjustment. Who you are in the home is who you really are, so don't think that your partner won't find out the *real* you in the early months and years of marriage. That's why you need to be consistent in your relationship to God; otherwise you will not have the right spiritual point of view to make the proper mental or physical adjustments.

Furthermore, you need to be aware of how living together under one roof places new pressures on newlywed couples. The compulsions of the intimacy of home living bring to the surface unplanned reactions to life's daily happenings. For example, if you have a tendency to air it out or scream or cry when you become tense or upset, I can guarantee you that your partner will soon discover your "hot buttons." How you react when those buttons are pushed will be an indication of whether you are reacting in a Christian way.

God says, "My grace is sufficient for you" (2 Corinthians 12:9, NKJV). Selfish reactions—such as "blowing a fuse" or pouting all weekend long—are an indication that you are not using this grace that God offers. For example, suppose your partner says something biting and unkind to you. Instead of receiving it graciously, you respond with your own torrent of abusive words. When that happens, you have sinned in God's eyes. Sure, your partner has sinned as well, but you are responsible to God only for your own sins.

If you act wrongly or verbally abuse your spouse, do not excuse your behavior, regardless of what prompted it ("She had it coming!"). Instead, you must humble yourself and go to God and confess your sin, asking him to give you a gracious spirit. Then tell your partner what you did, expressing regret for your actions or words.

Doing so helps us go through marriage—and life—with a clear conscience. The Holy Spirit gives us a conscience that helps us know when we have wronged him and others. We all blow it and say things we later regret; the key is to recognize those failures as sin and ask for God's forgiveness (1 John 1:9). In fact, those who face and confess their sin—and ask God for his help—will find that he provides a remedy.

You may be saying to yourself, *That's great, Tim, but I've always been taught to fight fire with fire. If my partner uses harsh and angry words with me, I'm not going to take that lying down.*

The Bible states that "a gentle answer turns away wrath" (Proverbs 15:1). It takes two to argue, so if you refuse to engage in discord, that ends the argument. Many family heartaches could be avoided if even one of the members would respond to God's guidance instead of following a scorched-earth policy. This illustration is only one of the many areas in which consistent actions according to God's principles will open up the way for happy marital adjustments.

Striving for Consistency

Consistency in the home is important. We do not have to be perfect to maintain the respect of our partner, but we should strive consistently to be who we say we are. If acting piously at the Sunday-morning church service, shaking hands with the preacher, and using all the right Christian lingo ("Have a blessed day") is followed by lashing out at your lover, telling little lies from sunup to sundown, and cheating on your expense reports, then you are acting like a hypocrite.

For this reason it is imperative for Christians to seek and follow God's directions for daily living. Thinking, talking, and acting in accordance with one's beliefs bring emotional peace as well as consistent behavior. Emotional peace will calm the waters of any turbulent marriage.

It is imperative to get your hypocrisy in check *before* children arrive. Once children are on the scene, they will be soaking up everything around them, especially in their home environment. If they witness their parents going through a whole lot of fussin' and feudin' during the week but acting like well-mannered, attentive Christian parents on Sundays, they will rightly figure that Christians are two-faced. They will not want to make your faith in Christ their own when they reach the teenage years.

Personal Devotional Life

Our spiritual vacuum is filled by the Holy Spirit when we accept God's provision for our soul: Jesus Christ. Jesus said, "I am the way, the truth, and the life. No one can come to the Father except through me" (John 14:6). When we ask Jesus Christ to direct our life, our spiritual life begins in earnest. We have access to God's help and direction, and this new spiritual element offers so much potential for personal change that the Bible says we are "born again." We were born first when we were born physically, and then we are born a second time when we accept spiritual life through Jesus Christ.

Taking care of our spiritual life is just as important as taking care of our physical life. God wants each of us to "grow in the grace and knowledge of our Lord and Savior Jesus Christ" (2 Peter 3:18, NKJV), and this growth comes only through the Word of God. Just as we feed our body three times a day, twenty-one times a week (whether we are famished or not), so must we daily feed our soul. Our spiritual food is the Word of God. Spending five to twenty minutes a day reading the Bible and meditating on God's words will help us live a consistent Christian life.

2. YOUR CHURCH LIFE

We immediately think of the church when we consider the spiritual area of life. Often people do not realize that spirituality is an intensely individual relationship with God. This relationship is not dependent upon the church, but it is definitely aided by the church. God desires that we come together to share our faith and worship him. The church should help people grow as Christians by giving us opportunities to study the Bible, by encouraging us to read Scripture and pray daily, and by giving us opportunities to serve and help other people.

Finding a church home is a snap for the young couple that has grown up in the same church. If, however, you were raised in different cities or have moved following the marriage, it will be necessary to find a church where both of you can feel at home and be enthusiastic participants. Each of you should give careful thought to what you want to give and receive from your church. My experience tells me that when a couple attends church haphazardly—without a definite purpose or goal—their spiritual lives wither on the vine.

What to Look for in a Church

When I was in the pastorate, I learned that 85 percent of the people who had joined our church came the first time because someone else invited them.

You want to join a church on more than a friend's recommendation, however. Your church home is so important that it should not be selected because of emotional sentiment or not wanting to hurt a friend's feelings. Instead, you should select a Bible-teaching church that has a solid reputation in spiritually training its congregation and young members. Here are some questions to ask yourself:

* Does this church teach out of the Bible? Does the minister preach from God's Word? Is the Sunday school material adequately based on Scripture? Can people meet each week for Bible study and prayer? I feel that it's so important to attend a Bible-teaching church that it would be better to change your denomination, provided it does not violate your doctrinal convictions, to attend such a church.
* Is this church concerned with helping other people find salvation in Jesus Christ? Does this church conduct occasional evangelistic campaigns? What is the church's evangelistic approach to the local community and the world at large?

* Is the church missionary-minded? A church that is not concerned with supporting missionaries often finds itself becoming a mission field. Ask about the missions committee and its commitment to spreading the Good News beyond our borders.

3. CHRISTIAN SERVICE AND WITNESS

Growing Christians want to serve Christ. Many young marrieds, however, get so involved in building a life together and establishing a home that they neglect Christian service. Those who fit that description have forgotten that Christ should still have first place in their lives (Matthew 6:33).

The early married years provide an excellent opportunity to serve others for Christ. If you think you're busy now, wait until the children come! Consider volunteering as a Sunday school teacher or even helping out in the nursery with the two-year-olds and three-year-olds. (Doing so will give you a foretaste of being around little ones!) As with everything else in the Christian life, we benefit by what we do for Christ. I have had many people approach me and say, "Pastor, since I have been teaching a Sunday school class, I have learned far more about the Bible than I ever learned from your sermons." That's great to hear. Christian service provides great motivation for studying the Word of God (2 Timothy 2:15), which in turn builds up one's Christian life.

Besides wanting us to serve in the church, Jesus Christ wants us to be involved in our communities. That means thinking, "What would Jesus say?" or "What would Jesus do?" when interesting conversations crop up at work or in your neighborhood. Don't be afraid to talk about your faith or to make it known that you attend a Christian church on Sundays. If a friend or acquaintance shows interest, talk about how Christ has changed your life. Sharing your faith with someone else will get you excited about your Christian walk. Jesus said that Christians are his witnesses to other people (Acts 1:8). People living empty lives need the dynamic witness of a Christian couple living in their midst.

4. SPENDING TIME WITH GOD

If you tried to live the whole week on a heaping Sunday supper, you'd be pretty hungry by Monday evening or Tuesday morning. In the same way, if you tried to live the whole week on the spiritual nourishment gained from a Sunday-morning worship service, you'd be pretty hungry to spend time with God by the first couple days of the work week.

We need spiritual food daily, and we gain that by reading the Bible, praying to our Lord, and learning more about him. This spiritual discipline is known as "devotions" or a "family altar" in some circles, but why not call it "time with Jesus" as you shoot for daily interaction with the God of the universe?

Spending time with God can be the single most powerful influence in the home, and its power is magnified when couples do it together. The couple who comes together already experienced in prayer knows the value and benefits of spending time with God. However, even if one or both partners are inexperienced at praying, the ideal place to learn the practice is with each other at home.

The Lord may well have had couples in mind when he gave us this promise: "I also tell you this: If two of you agree down here on earth concerning anything you ask, my Father in heaven will do it for you. For where two or three gather together because they are mine, I am there among them" (Matthew 18:19-20).

Devotions are not an ethereal or mysterious experience but a very simple and practical matter of reading the Bible and praying. The old adage "The family that prays together, stays together" is still true.

How to Have a Devotional Time

The following suggestions are offered to make your time with the Lord a meaningful experience.

* **Set a regular time for devotions, preferably morning, because reading the Bible and praying to God are a great way to begin the day.** If you are on different work schedules, discuss a time that works for both of you, even if it's after dinner or before you turn the lights out. The important thing is to start a practice that becomes a habit.

* **Read a passage of Scripture and, as you feel led, discuss what it means to you. Ask each other questions**. I highly recommend reading from the *Life Application Bible,* which comes with detailed notes on every page explaining God's Word in meaning and in context. A chapter a day would be an ideal goal. After the children arrive, you should read to them from some sort of "beginner's Bible."

* **Pray for others.** Be sure to uphold your missionaries regularly. Prayer should always carry the spirit of thanksgiving and feature the needs of unsaved neighbors, Christians who have fallen into sin, and the sick. Pray specifically so that you can receive specific answers. Write your prayers in a spiral notebook and watch how God answers them!

You will find that a devotional time with your spouse will provide a unique means of communication. Your partner will say things and share burdens that he or she would not be able to share on any other level. Praying together molds two people by the bonds and cords of love in a very thrilling way. United prayer is a way of multiplying and strengthening love through the passing years.

I'll never forget the time when a Christian man volunteered to me, "Tim, after twenty-six years of marriage, I am more sensitive to the thrill of her presence than I have ever been. When I see her unexpectedly in a crowd, a little song rises up somewhere inside me. When I catch her eye in public, it is as though she were hanging out a sign with the exact words of inspiration I needed right then. I still count it a thrill to see her each night after a long day. And as I look down the road ahead, I see us walking into the sunset hand in hand. I know in my heart that the end will be far better than the beginning."

Wasn't that wonderful? This couple had learned early in their marriage that God has a special plan for their lives, which includes their lifelong love for each other.

5. FORGIVENESS

We interrupt this book with an important news flash: You have not married a perfect person, and neither has your partner! Therefore, you'd better get used to forgiving your better half for mistakes, selfishness, and other forms of thoughtless behavior. (Hopefully, your spouse will see the importance of forgiving you as well.)

If you don't get into the forgiveness mode, you'll soon be carrying a grudge the size of an SUV. Let your watchword be Ephesians 4:31-32: "Get rid of all bitterness, rage, anger, harsh words, and slander, as well as all types of malicious behavior. Instead, be kind to each other, tenderhearted, forgiving one another, just as God through Christ has forgiven you."

God's Word says it all, doesn't it? An exacting person will find it more difficult to be forgiving than an easygoing person will. Nevertheless, God expects you to be forgiving. The Lord Jesus made that clear in Matthew 6:14-15 when he said that you cannot be forgiven of your sins unless you are willing to forgive others for theirs. Therefore, forgiveness is a spiritual necessity. You can be sure that your heavenly Father will enable you to do what he has commanded you to do—forgive one another regardless of the fault.

In closing, never go to bed angry! The Bible tells us, "Don't let the sun go down while you are still angry, for anger gives a mighty foothold to the Devil" (Ephesians 4:26-27). Your willingness to forgive your partner affects your spiritual life, both personally and as a family. Make it your responsibility to initiate forgiveness. Such a policy will help you achieve a spiritually strong home, which in turn will enrich every other area of your marriage. This includes the physical relationship, which we will discuss in the next chapter.

PHYSICAL 4 JOYS

THIS IS THE CHAPTER that almost couldn't be published in a Christian book thirty years ago. I'm glad it was included, and this chapter on marital sex is just as needed today as it was back then.

Physical adjustment in marriage can be properly compared to the instrumental adjustment necessary for the New York Philharmonic orchestra to produce a beautiful, harmonious symphony. Contrary to popular opinion, "doing what comes naturally" does not automatically guarantee physical harmony in the marriage relationship. Human beings are so much more complex in their emotional structure than animals that their sexual relationship cannot be compared to fulfilling the mating urge.

The "act of marriage," which is what I call the sexual act of married lovemaking, is the most thrilling experience a man and a woman can experience on this earth. If the act of marriage is not built upon mutual love and the climax of tender expressions of thoughtfulness and endearment, however, it will not produce the symphony of emotional harmony that God intended for married couples. Discordant notes in this area will lead to sexual frustration for one or both partners.

A lack of mutual harmony in the marriage relationship, however, does not mean that a marriage is doomed to failure. It just means that something is seriously wrong and that the couple should seek counsel from their pastor, doctor, or Christian counselor. Most sexual discord can be attributed to one of three things: ignorance, selfishness, or fear.

Having said that, let me be very frank in my presentation of the sexual relationship that exists between a husband and a wife. Some of this may sound like a repeat from a high school sex-ed class or one of those human-sexuality courses in college, but I would urge you to examine the following medical drawings and refamiliarize yourself with the names and functions of the various male and female reproductive organs. A proper understanding of these bodily functions will greatly aid your physical adjustment. Each organ is listed in the sequence of its reproductive function.

MALE REPRODUCTIVE ORGANS

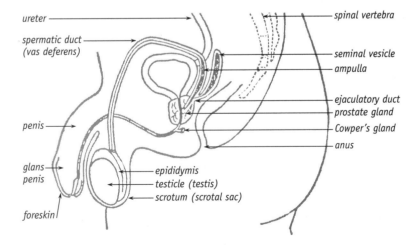

SCROTUM OR SCROTAL SAC—*the small pouch containing the testicles that hangs between a man's legs.*

TESTICLES—*the two sensitive, egg-shaped, sperm-manufacturing organs that hang in the scrotal sac. They contain a long, coiled tube, approximately one one-thousandth of an inch in diameter and about 1,000 feet long, and they can produce 500,000 sperm every week.*

SPERM OR SPERMATOZOA—*the male "seed" manufactured in the testicles. The sperm fertilizes the female egg. This seed contains the genetic information that determines the sex of the child. In the act of marriage, sperm are ejected through the penis into the vagina of the woman.*

EPIDIDYMIS—*the little channel in the scrotal sac where sperm manufactured in the testicles undergo a maturing process.*

SPERMATIC DUCT OR VAS DEFERENS—*the duct from the epididymis that carries the sperm into the ampulla chamber.*

AMPULLA CHAMBER—*the storage chamber for the sperm that have left the epididymis and traveled through the spermatic duct.*

SEMINAL VESICLE—*the organ producing the seminal fluid that carries the sperm to the prostate gland.*

EJACULATORY DUCT—*the organ that propels the sperm and seminal fluid through the penis into the vagina.*

PROSTATE GLAND—*this gland produces additional seminal fluid and contains the nerves that control the erection of the penis.*

COWPER'S GLAND—*when a man is sexually aroused, this is the first gland to function. This gland sends a few drops of slippery neutralizing* *fluid into the urethra, which prepares the urethra for the safe passage of sperm by neutralizing the acids of the urine that would otherwise kill the sperm.*

URETHRA—*the tube that carries urine from the bladder through the penis during urination. It also carries the sperm and semen from the prostate gland through the penis.*

PENIS—*the male sex organ through which both urine and sperm are released. Under usual conditions, the penis is very soft, spongy, and limp. When a man becomes sexually aroused, the penis is pumped with a large amount of blood that causes pressure, producing an erection that stretches the skin tight and makes the organ stand at an upward angle out from the body.*

GLANS PENIS—*the head of the penis, which is the most sensitive part of the organ. Friction on this area produces an ejaculation of sperm and seminal fluid.*

FORESKIN—*the loose skin that covers the glans penis for protection. In modern times, it has been the custom to circumcise, or cut away, this skin during infancy for hygienic purposes, a custom adopted centuries ago by Jewish people. A substance called smegma often gathers under the foreskin, producing an offensive odor. For this reason, the penis should be washed daily.*

AREAS OF SEXUAL SENSITIVITY—*the male genital organs, consisting of the penis, the scrotal sac, and the area around them, are exceptionally sensitive to touch. When caressed affectionately by the wife, they produce a pleasurable sexual excitement that prepares the husband for the act of marriage very quickly.*

NOCTURNAL EMISSION OR WET DREAM—*an involuntary ejaculation of semen during sleep. This can be an unsettling experience to a boy* *unprepared for it. If he awakens to find his pajamas wet and sticky, or hardened to a starchy consistency, he may be unnecessarily alarmed. What happens is that pressure builds up at a phenomenal rate from sperm manufactured by the testicles. The seminal vesicles are filled to capacity with fluid to a point where a man's entire reproductive system is waiting for release. Sometimes a dream during the night causes the penis to fill with blood, producing an erection. Cowper's gland puts forth its neutralizing drops of fluid into the urethra, and then the ejaculatory muscles and the sperm and seminal fluids are merged and spurt forth through the urethra and the penis. Teenage boys will experience many such nocturnal emissions.*

The constant production of sperm and seminal fluid is one reason why the man aggressively seeks release by making love. Again, these sexual urges are part of God's plan, so a husband's aggressiveness should be looked upon as the fulfillment of the God-ordained plan of mutual sexual fellowship between a husband and his wife.

● ● ● ● ● ●

The female reproductive system reveals the ingenious creative hand of God. The female organs are similar and complementary to the male reproductive system. This unique design will be revealed as you study the following organs and their functions.

OVARIES—*a woman has two ovaries, one on each side of her abdomen, located between her hip bones. These ovaries correspond to the male testicles and produce eggs. When a girl is born, her ovaries contain thousands of little eggs called ova. After a girl matures, her ovaries begin to secrete the female sex hormones that cause her to develop. Her breasts begin to enlarge, and hair grows under her arms and on her genital organs. Her hips begin to broaden, and she begins* *to take on a curvaceous, feminine appearance. At approximately one-month intervals, one of her eggs matures until it is about one two-hundredth of an inch in diameter, at which time it is released by the ovary into the fallopian tube.*

FEMALE REPRODUCTIVE ORGANS

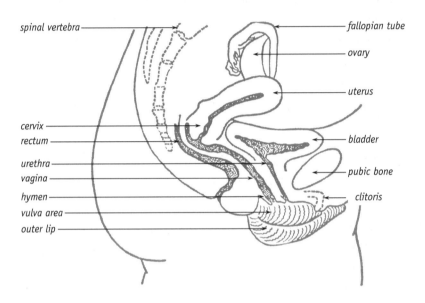

FALLOPIAN TUBES—*A woman has two fallopian tubes, one attached to each ovary. When the ovary releases an egg, the fallopian tube takes the egg to the uterus during a period of approximately seventy-two hours. If intercourse takes place during this period, it is quite probable that at least one of the active sperm will work its way through the vagina and uterus into the fallopian tube and will unite with the egg. At that moment, a human life is conceived. If the sperm in the fallopian tube does not fertilize the egg, the egg then passes into the uterus and dissolves.*

UTERUS OR WOMB—*the area in which the baby grows during pregnancy. This pear-shaped organ can be greatly expanded.*

VAGINA—*the primary female sex organ is comparable to the male penis and is designed to receive it. The vagina is made of soft, muscular tissue and provides a passageway from the outside of the body to the uterus.*

VULVA AREA—*the external opening to the vagina contains several organs, including the outer lips called labia majora. These lips are formed from the same kind of coarse skin as the scrotal sac of the male. Under sexual excitement, these lips swell or thicken. When these outer lips are opened, they reveal the inner lips called labia minora, which are very delicate membranes at the front of the vulva structure. These inner lips are made of skin very similar to the skin of the glans penis.*

CLITORIS—*a small organ just above the urethra near the entrance to the vagina. It is usually encased within the vulva skin and is similar in structure to the male penis. When a woman is sexually aroused, her clitoris will become firm and erect and will be sensitive to touch or body contact. It is the manipulation of this organ by contact with the penis, body, or fingers that produces the female orgasm. There are two types of female orgasm: clitoral and vaginal.*

AREAS OF SENSITIVITY—*a woman has more sensitive areas of sexual arousal than a man does. This is probably God's means of compensating for the fact that the husband often becomes more quickly aroused than his wife. Because a woman's breasts are very sensitive, affectionately caressing them helps to prepare her for sexual intercourse. When aroused, her nipples will often become hard and will protrude slightly, indicating proper stimulation. The large outer lips of the vulva area also become increasingly sensitive as they enlarge under arousal.*

The vagina and particularly the clitoris are also areas of sensitivity. When a woman is sexually aroused, several of her glands secrete a lubrication that bathes the vulva area and the vagina with a slippery mucus, easing the entrance of the penis into the vagina. This has nothing to do with fertility but is God's ingenious design for making the entrance of the penis a pleasurable experience for both the husband and the wife.

ORGASM—*the climax of a woman's emotional stimulus in the act of marriage is followed by a gradual decline in sexual stimulation, producing a warm sense of gratification and satisfaction. Although not the titanic, explosionlike experience of the male, the female's orgasm is just as gratifying; some female psychologists have suggested it is even more so.*

ATTITUDE

This explanation of the male and female reproductive organs prepares us for a discussion of attitude. One authority has stated, "Sex education is 20 percent education and 80 percent attitude." The right attitude is important for both husband and wife. The first thing to recognize is that sexual intercourse was designed by God for our good. When it occurs within the bonds of marriage, it could well be described as the most sublime expression of love between two people.

Because our overheated society makes such a big deal about sex, young Christian women aren't sure how to react if they come into marriage with their virginity intact. Are they supposed to act demure and reserved, or are they supposed to go hog-wild because all the restrictions are off? Sometimes, because of preconceived ideas or inappropriate relationships that went too far, young women feel a subconscious stab of guilt when making love. Or, their attitude about sex has been warped by a sexually frustrated mother who painted sexual intercourse as something akin to

Chinese water torture. They grew up believing that sex was dirty and should be avoided at all costs. These attitudes are contrary to God's plan, as you shall see. The following Scriptures amplify God's attitude toward sex:

> *The husband should not deprive his wife of sexual intimacy, which is her right as a married woman, nor should the wife deprive her husband. The wife gives authority over her body to her husband, and the husband also gives authority over his body to his wife. So do not deprive each other of sexual relations. The only exception to this rule would be the agreement of both husband and wife to refrain from sexual intimacy for a limited time, so they can give themselves more completely to prayer. Afterward they should come together again so that Satan won't be able to tempt them because of their lack of self-control.* 1 CORINTHIANS 7:3-5

> *So God created people in his own image; God patterned them after himself; male and female he created them. God blessed them and told them, "Multiply and fill the earth and subdue it. Be masters over the fish and birds and all the animals."* GENESIS 1:27-28

It is evident from these Scripture passages that the only taboos in the sexual relationship apply to sex outside the bonds of marriage. There is absolutely no connotation of evil involved in a proper relationship, as seen in Genesis 1:28, where God commanded Adam and Eve to bring forth children. This command was given before sin reared its ugly head (Genesis 3).

Happy are the man and woman who look upon the act of marriage as a means of showing their love in a special way that can never be shared with another person.

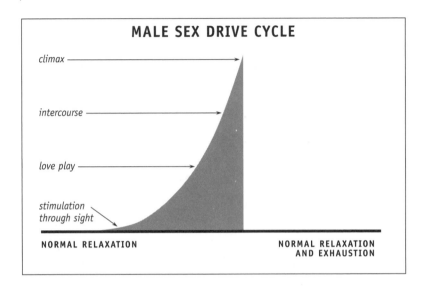

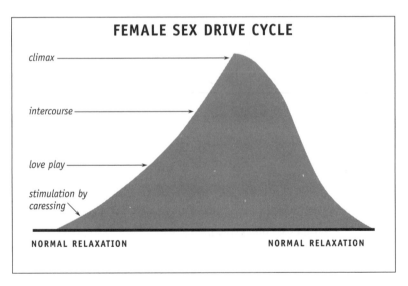

Emotional Differences

The differences between the reproductive systems of the
husband and the wife should stand as a symbol of the beautiful
differences in their emotional makeup. Failure to understand

these differences, particularly for the male, will prevent the complete satisfaction that God intended sexual intercourse to give to both partners.

The diagrams on page 54 will give you an idea of the emotional differences between men and women. Males are stimulated rather quickly and can proceed to intercourse and climax rapidly with very little or no foreplay. Once orgasm has taken place, men fall off the chart to a relaxed or exhausted state.

Women, on the other hand, need much more time—anywhere from ten to thirty minutes—to become fully aroused to the point where they can climax. This illustrates a vital difference between men and women. Author and speaker Gary Smalley says men heat up like microwave ovens but women are more like Crock-Pots when it comes to sexual response.

The emotional differences between the sexes begin with foreplay. Men, the way you engage in arousing your wife will make or break her enjoyment of lovemaking. Because men are often the initiators and women the receivers, you will have to watch for clues on how to proceed. This is done by both spoken and nonverbal cues. She can help you by expressing what she finds pleasurable and by placing your hands where she wants you to caress her tenderly. A thoughtful husband will gently massage his wife's neck, back, breasts, buttocks, and inner thighs. This will slowly build her arousal level, as seen in the graph.

As you take your time, you will build your wife's arousal to a point where she is ready to be touched in the vulval region. When she voluntarily spreads her legs, she is making her most sensitive area available for fondling. She is ready to be taken to the next step.

I believe that loving partners should incorporate manual clitoral stimulation into the act of marriage. This assures that she will receive an orgasm prior to penetration and that he will not feel pressure to hold off his ejaculation until his wife peaks, since many women do not reach orgasm during intercourse.

Clitoral stimulation involves the husband lying next to and slightly above his wife. As he tenderly caresses her clitoris and vaginal area with his fingers, he will sense when she is ready for him to gently insert a finger into the vagina. The husband can then start to make slow, rhythmic movements inside while the other fingers indulgently rub the outer vulval area, where the clitoris is located. As they move together, faster and faster, her breathing will become more rapid, and the experience will ultimately culminate in groans of orgasmic delight. Husbands find this exhilarating.

After she reaches orgasm, she will invite her husband to come into her, and they can delight in the act of marriage. Men, if you want to increase the number of times you make love, start by increasing the frequency of orgasm for your wife. You'll be amazed by how her appetite for lovemaking will increase.

A Personal Note to Husbands

There are several things that you, as a husband, should remember. One is that you must learn self-control in an effort to make your marriage relationship truly meaningful and enriched. As you know, you can receive physical satisfaction in lovemaking very simply and quickly, if need be. Nonetheless, if your wife does not experience satisfaction, then your marriage will not reach its maximum potential. Carefully consider these suggestions:

* **Women respond to tender affection and kind words.** Begin your love play when you see each other at the end of the day. Greet your wife with an affectionate kiss. With several

expressions of affection throughout the evening, your wife will be more prepared for the act of marriage when you go to bed.

* **Take a shower before retiring.** Slap some deodorant on, as well as her favorite cologne. Keep your fingernails trimmed, because you will use those to stimulate her clitoris and vulva area.

* **Know that God has given you a greater sex drive.** This means that she might not want to make love with you every evening and twice on Sunday night. Go with the flow.

* **A woman is usually "in the mood" during the middle of her menstrual cycle or just before or after her period, when her sex drive is particularly increased.** Occasionally some women have stronger sex drives than their husbands, or they will initiate sex. Although this is not common, this can be a rich blessing, since it is usually quite easy for a woman to inspire her husband to make love with her.

* **Refrain from using slang words and expressions for various sex acts.** By referring to the act of marriage with wholesome and endearing terms such as "making love," you elevate the physical act to the high and lofty heights that God intended.

* **After the thrilling consummation of making love, don't be in a hurry to withdraw from your wife.** Resist the temptation to turn over and fall asleep. Part of the satisfying effect for her is the physical closeness she feels with you after orgasm. Continue to touch and cuddle after your lovemaking experience.

* **Maintain good lines of communication with your wife so that you can talk freely about these delicate matters.** Frank discussions about what is most enjoyable to your partner will help you move toward a good physical adjustment.

A Personal Note to Wives

Your attitude toward making love is one of the keys that will unlock the door to marital happiness. It may surprise you to know that a poor attitude toward sex is the primary cause of low sexual desire among women. A significant amount of the female population, estimated to be 20 to 25 percent, go to their marriage bed each evening with an inhibited attitude toward sex. They view sex as a chore on a par with vacuuming and dusting.

A team of University of Chicago researchers, led by Edward Laumann, feels the number of women with low libido is higher. Writing in the *Journal of the American Medical Association*, the University of Chicago team said its research showed that 40 percent of women had very little interest in sex. This high figure doesn't seem possible in a sex-saturated society such as ours, but two of my doctor friends have confirmed this conclusion. They and counselors I've talked to say that most sexual problems aren't about sex but rather stem from conflict in other areas of marriage. Money problems, demanding infants and toddlers, and work- related problems can slam the brakes on sexual desire.

If you experience sexual dysfunction right off the bat in your marriage, don't postpone seeking help. Sit down with a counselor you know, such as a pastor. Don't worry, he's heard it all, and he should be able to impart some wise advice or steer you toward a professional counselor.

If I was sitting across the table from you, I would remind you that if a woman is frustrated in the act of marriage, something is wrong. God meant sex to be a mutually satisfying experience. Here are some other points I would make to help you approach this very important and meaningful part of your marriage:

* **Try to rid your mind of any prejudices or "old wives' tales" about making love.** Just because your mother was not well-adjusted in the physical area of marriage is no reason for you to perpetuate her mistakes and resultant misery. Approach the act of marriage with pleasurable anticipation. God meant it to be good!

* **Learn to make an exception to the wholesome standards of modesty and virtue that you have been taught.** Your husband should be the only exception! Premarital taboos sometimes are hard to forget, but with God's help you can forget them. When they are carried over toward your husband, they become a false standard of modesty. Do not be afraid to expose yourself to him. The more you can relax in his presence, the better you will adjust. This usually comes with time.

* **Daily bathing is highly recommended.** Take a shower before going to bed, although some suggest that a tub bath is preferable since the vaginal lubricants of the female anatomy can give off a strong odor.

* **Women are generally responders to their husband's affectionate expressions of love.** You can usually thoroughly enjoy the experience if you relax! At the same time, there is no law against you initiating sex with your husband. After you put smelling salts under his nose to bring him back to a conscious state, he'll be raring to go with you.

* **Take a wait-and-see approach.** Many a partner has gotten into the habit of stifling their spouse's advances with a tired sigh or the usual, "Not tonight, Honey. I have a headache." In doing so, she cheats them both out of a satisfying experience. Many a woman who responds to her husband's advances and goes on to make love is glad she did.

* **Talk about birth control.** If the fear of getting pregnant is keeping you from enjoying the act of marriage to its fullest extent, be sure to consult your doctor about a good birth-control program.

* **Don't be alarmed if you do not experience an orgasm during each sexual encounter with your husband.** If he doesn't bring you to a climax via manual clitoral stimulation, you can try to orgasm during intercourse by practicing the following suggestion. Since a man's climax is reached by the friction of the vagina against the glans penis, he is stimulated by his instinctive in-and-out motion. To delay this climax, the husband should stop his movement so that his feeling of imminent release will decline. If you remain immobile during this period, your emotions will also decline.

But the clitoris, which is the primary area that excites you to climax, is responsive to movements other than the in-and-out motions. When your husband stops, you can maintain the movement of his body against yours by slightly rotating or moving your hips, allowing you to rub your clitoris against his body. You may then continue building toward your emotional peak while he is waiting for his emotions to decline. When he resumes his instinctive movements, you will be able to climb together to your respective emotional peaks. It may be necessary for the husband to stop several times while the wife continues her climb through this very slight rotation technique. Concentration and practice will help couples to orgasm together, which is when the fireworks really begin!

Another thing you can do is to develop your vaginal muscles. As previously stated, a woman can experience a vaginal orgasm as well as a clitoris-produced climax.

Actually, the two should work together toward a climax. Since the muscles of the vagina, like other muscles of the human body, can be developed by exercise, you should attempt to tighten these muscles daily, both during intercourse and when lying in bed. Five to ten minutes of daily flexing and tightening these muscles strengthens them and increases the capacity for sexual stimulation, thus assisting your ability to reach an orgasm.

Sometimes you will find that one or two days a month, according to your reproductive cycle, things that ordinarily cause great emotional stimulus actually work in reverse. Instead of increasing your sexual ardor, they actually dispel it and, in some cases, make you irritable. Don't be deceitful during these occasions. Sometimes it is best not to engage in marital sex at this time; other times, by limiting your preliminary love play to kissing, your physical relations can be consummated. Although it is still a rewarding experience, you will not find sex to be the exhilarating and exciting experience that it has been on other occasions.

* **Keep the lines of communication on these matters open between you and your husband so that there is no misunderstanding.** Most natural differences can be ironed out. A happy physical adjustment will happen if two people talk frankly about their love life.
* **If you find that the sexual relationship becomes a chore without enjoyment or meaning, seek the advice of a Christian counselor.** God has better things for you.

A final note to men and women: If you will be getting married soon or are in the early years of marriage, you should consider reading *The Act of Marriage*, a biblically-based sex education resource that Bev and I wrote in 1976 and that was revised and updated several years ago. Today, more than 2.5 million copies are in print. Thousands of people have written us to express their appreciation for the way we dealt right up front with the meaning and importance of good sex. We especially liked hearing from couples who had received a copy during premarital counseling sessions with their pastor or from some mature Christian they respected. Nothing made us happier than to read those letters.

Take Your Time, Buster

An evangelist friend of mine told me a story that shows our heavenly Father's interest in one couple's maladjusted physical relationship. While my friend was holding a week of meetings in a certain city, a young husband he had led to Christ some years before insisted my friend stay at their home. This man was very successful in the business world and well respected in the Christian community. He and his wife had two wonderful children and gave the impression of being the ideal couple. Little did the evangelist dream that these two wonderful people had a serious problem.

After breakfast the first morning, the minister casually said to the wife, "How are things going?" She turned from the sink where she was working and tearfully cried, "Oh, Keith, I'm so miserable!" She then related how completely frustrated she was in their physical relationship because her dynamic husband approached her with the same overpowering enthusiasm that he used for everything in life. Consequently, she felt used rather than loved. She had been praying that God would somehow help them in their sexual relationship.

That night as the minister was getting ready for bed, he stepped into the bathroom to brush his teeth. The bathroom happened to be located between the two bedrooms, and while my friend was brushing away, he couldn't help but hear the bed squeak and his friend grunt and groan as he "made love." The entire episode was over in three minutes! This slam-bam sex was nothing more than physical satisfaction of the masculine mating urge.

The next morning, the evangelist asked his friend to stay home from work, and they talked in the backyard for two hours. To the minister's amazement, his friend, a college graduate who dearly loved his wife, didn't even know anything was wrong. Neither of these young people had read a book on the subject of sex, and they had never been given marriage counseling. When the preacher finished the long-overdue counseling session, the young man was heartbroken. He confessed his selfishness to God and asked for divine wisdom in being the kind of husband that God wanted him to be, one that "loved his wife as his own body."

Six months later the evangelist met this couple at a banquet. During the evening the wife turned to him and said, "I can't thank you enough for what you have done for us. Our whole marriage has been transformed." My friend told me, "The look of joy on her face reminded me again that God is interested in every area of the Christian's life, including the physical adjustment."

Christian couples can have the best possible physical relationship in marriage, even if they start out as complete novices. God is interested in every area of life, including this very important relationship. He can guide you to the right book or the proper counselor. Remember, God considers the act of marriage as the supreme expression of love between two human beings.

SUGGESTED ADDITONAL READINGS:

Douglas E. Rosenau, M.D., *A Celebration of Sex* (Thomas Nelson, 1996).

Clifford L. Penner, Ph.D., and Joyce J. Penner, R.N., M.N., *Getting Your Sex Life Off to a Great Start* (Word, 1994) and *The Gift of Sex* (Word, 1982).

Ed Wheat, M.D., and Gaye Wheat, *Intended for Pleasure* (Revell, 1997).

Tommy Nelson, *The Book of Romance* (Thomas Nelson, 1998).

Archibald D. Hart, Ph.D., Catherine Hart Weber, Ph.D., and Debra L. Taylor, M.A., *Secrets of Eve: Understanding the Mystery of Female Sexuality* (Word, 1998).

ADJUSTING 5 TO CHILDREN

Mark and Missy sitting in a tree,
K-i-s-s-i-n-g
First comes love, then comes marriage.
Then comes Missy pushing a baby carriage!

REMEMBER THAT OLD RHYME from your schoolyard days? Those four lines seem rather quaint these days in a society that celebrates its cultural icons' having children out of wedlock. We live in an age when Madonna and her first child are plastered on *People* magazine and held up as role models for the "new family."

It's too bad the Material Girl does not see the wisdom contained in that childhood ditty. The nursery rhyme tells a simple story: Mark and Missy get to know each other, fall in love, get married, and have children. They are following a sequence that makes sense in a Dr. Laura sort of way. Today's entertainment media, however, calls that square. They say it's sometimes better—and easier—to raise children without a father in the home, and if you do get married, nobody expects the union to last. They have it all wrong, but there's one thing we can all agree on: The desire to have children and raise them is a primordial instinct as deep as the ocean is wide.

Perhaps you've perceived the motherhood urge in recent

months. You felt that lump in your throat when your brother presented you with his first child and let you hold her close in your arms. As you think these wistful thoughts, realize that your child- hood experiences influence your desire for children. If you enjoyed a good home life and a stable home environment, you will probably look upon children as a blessing. If you experienced a wretched childhood that you wouldn't wish upon your worst enemy, you may not desire children. However, I have seen many people who used their disadvantaged background as a stimulus to provide their offspring with something better than they had.

WHERE DOES TEMPERAMENT FIT IN?

Temperament often plays a bigger part than background in deter- mining a person's desire for children. Mr. and Mrs. Sanguine invari- ably want children, which makes sense because they love people. Mr. and Mrs. Choleric often desire children because they need someone to provide for or some "project" to keep them busy. However, they may be reluctant to have children because they are so busy working that they don't want to be encumbered by little folks.

Mr. and Mrs. Melancholy are so indecisive and perfectionism prone that they may vacillate for years, often waiting until it's too late before deciding to have children. Mr. and Mrs. Phlegmatic usually desire children because they are friendly, good-natured folks who want to do the accepted thing.

The decision to have children shouldn't be based on what temperament God gave you, how much money is in your joint checking account, or whether you will need to move into a bigger home. Those things have a way of working out. Your decision to "try" should begin with prayer as you and your spouse seek God's will and blessing upon your effort.

Following prayer, you should discuss your feelings and make plans based on the answers to the following questions:

* When shall we stop using birth control?
* Will she become a stay-at-home mother, or does she want to continue her career? Can we live off one income? If not, what does it cost to send the mother back into the workforce?
* How many children would we like to have? How far apart?
* Will we have to move into a larger home? If so, how much will that cost?

If a mother decides to have children and return to the workplace, she will, in some ways, be giving her child to someone else to raise. I strongly urge you not to take that route. Besides, when you deduct the tax withholding, cost of day care, wear and tear on the second car, a work wardrobe, and extra meals eaten out (because both parents are too tired to cook), most "working moms" rarely *net* more than five dollars per hour. Wouldn't you rather lower your lifestyle a bit and raise that special child that the Lord gave *you* to raise? Put another way, don't you want to instill *your* values into your children and not leave that to someone else (who could be a stranger)?

God has mercifully given babies an uncanny ability to work into almost any parent's heart and carve out a special place of love. Rare indeed is that parent who can look his infant in the face and say, "I wish you had never been born." Instead, many who hesitated on the threshold of parenthood have responded to the parental instinct once their child drew his first breath. In this day when planning or delaying a family is being overemphasized, too many young couples are likely to cheat themselves out of one of life's most enriching experiences: being a mom and dad.

CHILDREN: NOW OR LATER?

The trend of indefinitely delaying a family is part of the cultural landscape. With the advent of various methods of birth control, "planned parenthood" has become a reality. The problem is, most couples feel they must wait until they can "afford" children before trying to become parents. As I mentioned earlier in the section about financial adjustments, it is easy to fall into the rut of an exaggerated standard of living in the early days of marriage when both the husband and wife are working. Most men never increase their earning power to equal their combined incomes—or if they do, it takes so many years that the wife is long past her childbearing age.

This waiting-until-we-can-afford-children attitude concerns me because often the waiting is caused by a selfish desire for a high standard of living. The couple never finds the joy and satisfaction from material things that they would have found in having children. If only you could have been sitting in my counseling office when I listened to a childless couple pour out their hearts to me. Said one distraught woman, "We waited until we could afford children, and now we can't have them."

The Ideal Childbearing Age

When my wife, Bev, went into labor with our third child, Lee, we thought the delivery would be a piece of cake. After all, she had given birth to two children with no complications at all.

When Bev's labor did not progress, however, the doctor informed us that he would have to do a cesarean section.

"Why a cesarean?" I asked the doctor.

"This baby probably weighs nine or ten pounds, and that's what's holding things up."

"How can that be?" I asked. "Our first two children weighed more than that." Bev had given birth to two *large* babies.

"Well, Tim, Bev's not as young as she used to be."

"But Doctor, she's only twenty-five years old!"

"I know," he said, shaking his head. "Most women are physically prepared to have children when they approach twenty years of age. From then on their ability to bear diminishes each year."

I thought of that story because so few women understand that the ideal childbearing age is shorter than most people think and does not necessarily parallel today's customs. I can state that if you have children in your twenties, both you and your child will face fewer risks. It's a known fact that older women have a higher percentage of children born with birth defects such as Down's syndrome and spina bifida. *But isn't having children in your twenties too young? Shouldn't you wait until you're older and more mature?*

What young couples lack in maturity they gain in energy. Mothers and fathers in their twenties have better physical skills to cope with sleepless nights, round-the-clock feedings, and boisterous toddlers. Yet this is not what you hear from today's society, which has been telling women for the last thirty years that "you can have it all"—marriage, career, and children—anytime you want it. In addition, the emphasis on careerism is rampant. Women are being instructed to delay marriage by "starting a career" or going on to graduate school or some advanced form of schooling.

Once they're firmly established in the workforce, then they can think about "settling down" and marrying. This often isn't until their late twenties or early thirties. When they finally do reach the altar, they're urged to take several years "settling in," which takes them into their midthirties. By this time, a woman's biological clock is ticking VERY LOUDLY, and she may be scrambling to become pregnant. I can assure you that it is far more difficult for a woman to get pregnant at thirty-five than it is at twenty-five or younger.

While I'm on the topic of young marriages, let me offer a personal story. Bev was eighteen years old when we married; I was twenty-one. I realize that we married in a different day and age, but I'm glad we married young. I wouldn't trade that experience for anything today.

Bev and I continued to go to college after the nuptials, but then she got pregnant during her sophomore year. I don't know whether it was the cold winters in Minnesota, but she became pregnant again within a year. We eventually became parents of four children, and Bev was a great mom. When she reached her early forties, the children were off to college, so she decided to come back into the workforce as a college registrar. Bev wrote several books, and when she was fifty years old, she founded Concerned Women for America, which grew to become the largest women's organization in the country.

One day I was sitting in Bev's office in Washington, D.C., where she headed an organization with forty full-time employees. "Honey, one of the things that amazes me about you is that you are such a good manager, but you have never taken a management course. You seem to have the ability to paint the big picture, give assignments, and check up on people in a gracious way. Why is that?"

"That's easy to answer," said Bev. "You can't raise four children without being a good checker-upper."

Our society depreciates the incredible lessons a woman can learn in the home as she raises children. Mothers become good "checker-uppers"—a great management skill. As long as a mother continues to read a variety of materials, she will be educated. For those career-oriented women, let me remind you that jumping off the career carousel is something you will never regret. Motherhood is a season of life that travels all too quickly. Don't let that season pass you by. You can always jump back on that carousel when the children go off to college.

Let me finish this section by imparting some advice to parents of young adults: Mom, Dad—be willing to help out your young adults financially. When I was young, most parents said this to their offspring as they bade them good-bye following high school graduation: "I will help put you through college, but if you get married, I stop paying for school." That is a stupid philosophy. Why shouldn't parents continue to help a young couple that marries while they are still in school? You are making an investment in your children that will better their lives and help them earn degrees that can put them on the path to better-paying jobs and a brighter future.

I think it's far better for a young Christian man and woman, who are in love and who have sought the Lord's will, to marry while they are still in college than to wait until they graduate. For a parent to support their education bills at this time is a gift that knows no bounds. I also believe, for similar reasons, that parents who help a married son or daughter with the down payment on a first home are doing themselves and their child a tremendous good.

REARING CHILDREN

What are the qualifications of a good parent? You do not have to be a college graduate, for history reveals that some of the greatest men and women had unlettered parents. It doesn't take riches, charm, or natural gifts. I can sum up the requirements for parenthood in one word—*maturity.* Any young couple mature enough to live unselfishly with each other is qualified to be parents. All children need is unselfish parents! The parents' adjustments as to whose responsibility it is to get up at night, whose responsibility it is to change the diapers, etc., can easily be set when approached with love and unselfishness.

I do not pretend to be an authority on rearing children, but two basic areas of responsibility that I want to present are love and training. Although they are inseparable and should be administered jointly, I shall discuss them separately.

LOVE

Nearly all psychologists and child specialists agree that love is basic to proper development for every human being. A parent's love is more important to children than wealth or education or any form of material possessions. When children bask in the security of their parents' love, they gradually develop a wholesome outlook toward life. The home may fall far short of perfection in many areas; this lack will serve to prepare the children for life in an imperfect world. But in order for them to have a positive mental attitude, the one thing they must never lack is love.

For this reason, parents must be careful to show love even as they administer corrective discipline. Overly critical, domineering parents produce fear-prone children. Even the most strong-willed children can be made indecisive if they are constantly harassed, criticized, and browbeaten by their parents. Perfectionist-prone parents must be careful not to foist their perfectionist standards on their child but to make them feel securely loved. Thoughtful parents can convey the thought to their child that although they do not approve of a particular action, they nonetheless approve of the child and love him or her. After all, loving correction is the way our heavenly Father treats us: "For the Lord disciplines those he loves, and he punishes those he accepts as his children" (Hebrews 12:6).

The Bible contains two commands to children. Ephesians 6:1-2 says that children must *obey* their parents and *honor* them. It would be nice if children would automatically do this for their parents, but if parents don't lovingly demand that their children obey and honor them, they won't. Rebellion is bound in the heart of children, but Proverbs says that "discipline will drive it away" (Proverbs 22:15).

I spanked my children when they were very young and had willfully disobeyed me, and they have grown up and become parents who have, in turn, practiced "loving corporal punishment" with their children. "Dad, you were right," they say. My adult children understand that when a child wants to run into the street, a loving spank will teach him not to do that, which could save his life.

You see, God put a nerve from the seat of the pants to the top of the brain that, when lovingly tapped, sends a message. Children have to learn obedience because there is no such thing as total freedom. For example, we Americans think we have the freest highway system in the world, but we do not have the freedom to make a U-turn in a four-lane freeway. Obeying the law increases freedom, not decreases it.

The discipline of children should begin early in life. Sometimes I meet a mother or father who weakly says, "I love my children too much to spank them." That is not true; that is a maudlin attitude. One of the most difficult things to do is to discipline your children. But it must be done. Don't shirk your duties! Your children need you to set limits and teach them the right behavior.

You Cannot Give Too Much Love

The one thing that you cannot give too much of to your children is love. Children need to be reassured by their parents of their love, but then, isn't that true for you as well? Who doesn't enjoy hearing from his or her partner those magic words: "I love you!"

Fathers should be particularly careful to shower their daughters with affection. Most men do not realize the importance of extending this affection to their young girls. The serious consequence of an inadequate father-daughter relationship was impressed upon me years ago while talking with my wife's gynecologist. We both did a lot of counseling work, so I asked him about a problem that was on my mind: "Has medical science come up with a pill that will cure frigidity?"

He laughed and said, "Not to my knowledge! The best preventive medicine for that problem that I know of is an affectionate father."

Since then, when counseling women who have a problem finding pleasure in sex, I have inquired about their relationship with their father. Invariably, I hear a story of how they feel they were rejected since earliest childhood. Another possible cause of frigidity can be a traumatic experience such as child molestation that leaves an emotional scar and prevents a young woman from feeling relaxed in the presence of her husband.

Transferal of Love

When a little girl comes to her dad to be loved and is rejected, this rejection leaves a lasting scar upon her subconscious mind. If her father never has time for her, never is interested in her drawings, or does not let her sit on his lap or feel free enough to put her arms around his neck, then in all probability she will develop a protective resistance to her father's rejection to avoid being continually hurt.

Since her first masculine image is that of her father, she is prone to transfer this image to all men, including her husband.

Whatever resentment and hostility she has been fostering in her heart against her father is often transferred to her husband. This faulty but natural conditioning process will set up a young woman for a less-than-ideal marriage and can be avoided by a thoughtful father who recognizes that every little girl needs to be loved by the one man in her life who is most important to her—her dad.

All of this talk about father-daughter affection does not mean that little boys are not also in need of love from their fathers and mothers. The above analysis simply illustrates one of the sad consequences of the lack of love. Many abnormal actions of today's adults can be traced to the simple fact that when they were children, they were never assured of their mother's or father's love.

Fortunately, this devastating blow to a person's emotional nature can be cured by the power of Jesus Christ. God in his marvelous grace offers us the Holy Spirit to supply the peace, joy, love, and faith that all human beings need to have an adequate feeling of security, regardless of whether or not their parents loved them. But until they go to the Holy Spirit for help, they will experience many unnecessary fears, doubts, and limitations because they didn't receive the love they needed.

Some parents have to work harder than others to express their love because of their natural temperament and childhood experiences. A father I know committed what I considered a terrible blunder one day. His thirteen-year-old daughter skipped up to him in the exuberant effervescence of youth and spontaneously reached out to kiss him. His involuntary reaction was to turn his lips away, so she kissed him on the cheek. It just happened that when his face turned, her eyes were looking straight into mine, and I saw that momentary look of disappointment on her face.

Deciding that his daughter's emotional development was worth risking our friendship, I later talked to the father about this incident.

Fortunately, he took my suggestion the right way and admitted it was difficult for him to show affection, particularly if he thought anyone would be observing the exchange. As gently as I could, I pointed out that he was hindering his daughter's emotional development—and putting her future relationship with her husband at risk.

Doing and Not Doing

Spanking is not the only means of discipline, and besides, most parental spanking should be finished by the time children reach first or second grade. Like most parents, due to youthful ignorance, we probably spanked our first child more than the other three combined. As we became more experienced at this game called parenting, we learned that there were other ways of using discipline that were equally effective—from sitting on the bed ten to thirty minutes, depending on the crime, to taking away the keys to the family car.

One thing we should learn about administering discipline is that we never have to lose our temper and discipline our children in anger. Some parents tend to use spanking as a means of releasing their own pent-up frustrations at their children's actions. One of the necessary things to remember in discipline is consistency, but many parents end up spanking their children because the parents have been inconsistent with discipline. They will tell their son, "Now, Junior, don't do that" and forget that one minute after hearing "Don't do that," Junior will put them to the test to see whether or not they mean it. This is the time to recognize what is happening and to stay the discipline course.

A good suggestion that will help you avoid inconsistency is this: Don't forbid your children anything unless you really mean it. Then if they test you, make sure you pass the test. We found by trial and error what seemed to us to be a good method for dealing with those infractions of family rules that demanded spanking. We used a wooden spoon, probably because that was what I was reared on. The first time our children did something that was forbidden, they got one spank on the behind with the spoon; for the second infraction, they received two spanks; for the third, they received three, and so on. For some reason, it was never necessary to give more than three for a given offense. The secret to this, or any form of discipline, is consistency.

Children quickly learn that parents have different ideas in certain areas of discipline. They immediately begin to exploit these differences by pitting one parent against the other. The solution to this problem is like the solution to all the others—loving communication. Most couples do not establish set standards of behavior. Instead, they try to deal with every crisis as it comes up. It is much better to set guidelines and stick to them; children are more comfortable when discipline is consistent.

Both parents should agree that when one speaks, both have spoken; thus, they will avoid the dilemma of the child who disobeys dad with mother's permission. That does not mean you will always agree with your spouse's interpretation of the rules. Any disagreements, however, should be reserved for a discussion with your partner behind closed doors. If one agrees that he or she has made a mistake, then that parent should be the one to correct it. The idea is to maintain unity before the children.

TRAINING

The best educational institution in the world is the home. Today's society has defaulted on this opportunity and tries to make the school, the media, and sometimes the church do training that ideally should occur in the home. This shifting of responsibility has proven to be inadequate. Outside the home and the church, lessons and programs tend to have weak or entirely absent moral principles and standards of behavior.

Moral behavior standards have been in a free fall since the 1960s. The idea of an absolute standard—known as absolute truth—has been rejected by much of today's society. The new buzzword is tolerance: *You do your thing, and I'll do mine.* Contemporary Americans seem to be more comfortable living in gray areas, where right and wrong are not clear-cut. They have adopted a policy of "moral relativity," which means that you have no more right to say what's right or wrong than I do. For example, you may feel that abortion is wrong, but that's just a manifestation of "your morality."

The Bible provides a standard of right and wrong. Instead of apologizing for it, we should teach it to our children line upon line, precept upon precept (Isaiah 28:10). The Bible says, "Don't copy the behavior and customs of this world, but let God transform you into a new person by changing the way you think" (Romans 12:2). If you want the perfect will of God for your children, then it is your responsibility to teach God's way of thinking to them.

The Teen Years

Children grow up rapidly, shedding their youth-choir countenance for a cantankerous demeanor—also known as *adolescence*—seemingly overnight. After years of cheery, sweet behavior, they challenge you at every turn and seek their peers' advice for everything from what clothes to wear to what classes to take at school.

You may wonder what happened to your children when they reach the teen years. Understand that turmoil is a typical transition from childhood to adolescence. The final third of your parenting years is the most crucial stage, however. Lose them now, and you could lose them forever.

It's not my intention to scare you. I prefer to see the teen years in a positive light because these can be the *best* years of your lives together. It's exciting to watch your offspring mature into godly young adults, full of hope and vim for a future that looks boundless to them. What I'm saying is that these are not the years to be AWOL—absent without leave—or to abdicate your parental role due to busyness, indifference, laziness, or a lack of desire to engage your teens. Teens need you more than ever before, although they would never tell you that. Don't be afraid to step in and offer parental leadership, even if you're not sure what to do or you believe that you long ago lost the upper hand with your children. Parent in such a way that you come alongside your teens; don't parent in some top-down, managerial way.

This leads me to make an important point: *You'll lose your teens if you don't know their world.* Unless you're aware of what's on their radar screens, you will not be able to relate to them and their world. Unless you know about all the media coming at them (Hollywood films, TV shows, music, instant messaging, MP3), you will not know what's being whispered in their ears. This doesn't mean you have to watch every teen-targeted movie, listen to their favorite CDs, spike your hair, or wear short skirts (by the way, teens *hate* parents who adopt their fashions), but you do need to understand where they are coming from.

The Music Scene

Much of the teen world revolves around music. When I originally wrote *How to Be Happy Though Married,* rap, hip-hop, heavy metal, speed metal, and alternative music hadn't even been *invented.* These days, practically every teen in America hears this type of music because it's in your face. Popular music has morphed into a frenetic, bass-driven sound accented by raunchy lyrics that are played so loudly and so often that no one blushes anymore.

Rap music is one of the worst offenders. Rappers, in their stylized monotone, jive-talk about "bustin' hos" and employ street terms to describe oral sex, anal sex, and rape. They put down anything that's good, and they glorify cop killing and drug dealing. Kids lap it up because it's antiauthority.

Of course you don't want your teens to listen to this stuff, but the area you want to emphasize with your teens is *content,* not style. Your issue with popular music should not so much be the beat but what the lyrics say. If you're zapping through channels with your family and you stop on MTV long enough to say, "Look at those guys. They look like girls!" or the infamous "I can't understand the words," all you've done is reveal your prejudices or your age.

Instead, you should introduce your teens to great gospel and CCM artists. CCM, which stands for Contemporary Christian Music, has tons of groups and singers in nearly every genre—rap, pop, rock, metal, ska, and techno. Some CCM artists are very "edgy," but you can count on positive lyrics that lift up rather than bring down your kids.

Set Limits and Definite Rules

It isn't always easy to set limits and define rules for your children and teenagers, but it certainly pays. Sometimes they will argue and fight over the rules you establish, but they secretly appreciate them. Good training involves explaining rules to teens, but there may come a time when no amount of reasoning will make them joyfully accept their parents' decision. Don't be deterred by their objections; set good rules whether your teens like them or not.

The old adage of "actions speak louder than words" is never

truer than during the teen years. The best sermons your children will ever hear are the ones they see you live. If you have a lackadaisical attitude and a scattershot record of attending church on Sunday, your teens are taking notes. If you're drinking beer every time a ball game is on TV, your teens are certainly going to think that regular drinking is okay. Christian parents should adopt the standard of behavior set by the apostle Paul, who said to his spiritual sons and daughters, "You should follow my example, just as I follow Christ's" (1 Corinthians 11:1).

The adolescent years are a difficult time for young people, because as new opportunities and responsibilities come their way, teens often don't have enough insight or experience on which to base decisions—like listening to the right music. They are frequently faced with crossroad situations. Should they listen to their friends? Should they do something that contradicts their moral standards? Many of their decisions and actions today affect— either negatively or positively—their future. Commit them to God, trusting him, as the Bible teaches in Psalm 37, to protect them through this tempestuous phase of life.

When life is over and we look back, the greatest joy that can fill our heart is to be able to say with the apostle John, "I have no greater joy than to hear that my children walk in truth" (3 John 1:4, NKJV).

SIX KEYS TO MARITAL HAPPINESS

THE PUNDITS TELL US that we live in the Information Age, a time when an explosive amount of information is available to us at our fingertips. Log on, and you can click through millions of pages on the World Wide Web devoted to the topic of marriage—free for the taking. Turn on the TV late at night, and you can stumble upon an infomercial extolling the virtues of "building a strong relationship," available in three easy-to-watch videos for the low, low price of $99.95.

One of the positive aspects of this mushrooming development is that Christian bookstores—which were practically nonexistent when I got married in the late 1940s—have sprouted like May flowers across the fruited plain. Young couples stepping into these retail establishments will find an unprecedented amount of biblically based material, ranging from books to videos to cassette tapes to CDs.

Perhaps that's why you're holding this book in your hands—you're desiring to enrich your marriage. You've come to the right spot, and in keeping with the times (which like advice and information presented in quick spurts), I'm going to present six keys that are guaranteed to open the door to a happy marriage.

Examine each key carefully. The degree to which you use them will determine the success of your marriage. If you neglect them, your marriage cannot help but be a miserable and wretched experience. If you incorporate these keys into your marriage, however, you have an excellent chance to develop a deeper intimacy that too few couples ever attain. These keys come from the Bible, God's manual on human behavior. Therefore, I can guarantee happiness and success to all who use them.

KEY #1: MATURITY

The first key that guarantees happiness in marriage is maturity. This key is best defined in the emotional realm as unselfishness. Do you have the maturity to take the long view? To delay gratification? To realize that marriage is a marathon, not a sprint?

Hopefully, you have not married someone who is immature—the grown-up version of a child who threw fits in a supermarket, lying on the floor kicking and screaming because Mommy wouldn't buy a favorite candy bar. Immature kids can grow into immature young adults who still pout and demand their way in practically every situation. Such attitudes, which are subtle and difficult to recognize (especially when both partners are immature), are often disastrous to a marriage.

The Problem

The adjustment stage of marriage, usually considered the first three years, can be counted on to produce conflicts of interest. Think about it: As young people enter high school and move on to college and their first jobs, they have been living more and more independent lives. They are used to making decisions purely on the basis of what they want or what is best for themselves. After the wedding, however, two independent individuals must learn to mesh together. Since they are both moving objects, and all movement creates friction, there is bound to be friction until they learn to move together in unity.

A good illustration of friction is the manual transmission. Yes, I know I am showing my age since many young people have never driven a stick-shift car, but here's how the analogy goes: As long as the car stands still without the motor running, you can press in the clutch and move the gear shift, meshing different gears at will, without problems. Once you turn the ignition, however, things change rapidly. Young drivers, unaccustomed to a manual transmission, grind or "clash" the gears as they shift from first to second gear in an effort to increase speed. It is only through concerted effort and practice that inexperienced drivers learn to shift smoothly from one gear to the next.

The gears of marriage grind in the early years when both partners are immature and selfish. Imagine two newlyweds sitting in a VW Beetle. He is sitting in the driver's seat; she is sitting shotgun—and both are trying to shift the gear knob! I often saw similar discordant clashes in my counseling office as I listened to selfish newlyweds wonder why they were having such a hard time "adjusting" to marriage. They were stuck in first gear—or reverse!

The increase in people's immaturity and selfishness has been perhaps the biggest cultural shift I have seen in my lifetime. It certainly has become a huge problem in all interpersonal relationships, especially marriage. The elevation of selfishness to what psychologists call a "right" has caused a sea change. Instead of going into a marriage relationship with a desire to serve and help their partner live a fulfilled life, people are going into marriage asking, "What can I get out of it?" Couples do not have a servant mentality, nor do they have the slightest inclination to learn what servanthood is all about. This is a manifestation of immaturity. On the flip side, if two mature people come together in marriage, their spirit of selflessness will make it very easy for them to adjust.

You Never Get by Getting

I'll never forget counseling one youthful bride who arrived in tears. Her husband was unfeeling and seemed to be caught up in himself, she said. My sixth sense told me that *she* had been just as selfish as her new husband, but she wasn't ready to hear that opinion. So I talked at length about the importance of giving in a marriage.

A light went on in her head. "Your advice is sure different from the advice the girls at the office gave me," she said. "My friends told me, 'Madeline, don't give too much of yourself to your husband; he'll just take advantage of you. One thing to remember in marriage is that men are out for all they can get.'" That unchristian and unsound attitude is one of the things that produces so much misery in American homes.

In God's economy, you never get anything by getting. The way to get something is to give it away. If you want love, for example, don't look for it—give it. If you want friends, don't look for friends—be friendly. The same is true of thoughtfulness, consideration, and selflessness. If you want your partner to treat you unselfishly, then be mature enough by God's grace to treat that special person unselfishly. Of the thousands of people I've counseled over the years, I've never counseled anyone who was "outgiving" the other person, but I've sure had to counsel those who were acting selfishly.

Why did you get married in the first place? The answer to that question may give you an insight into your maturity. Did you get married because "I had an unhappy home life" or because "I got tired of my parents telling me what to do" or because "All my friends were getting married, and I didn't want to be left alone" or because "I wanted somebody to love me"? The proper attitude that guarantees success in a marriage is based on mature unselfishness. Mature individuals will go into marriage not only for what they can get out of it, but also for what they can give to their partner. Two verses in the Bible come close to being a magic wand; when used by marriage partners, they turn chaos into peace and harmony:

> *Let nothing be done through selfish ambition or conceit, but in lowliness of mind let each esteem others better than himself. Let each of you look out not only for his own interests, but also for the interests of others.* PHILIPPIANS 2:3-4, NKJV

If you go into marriage with this attitude—"Don't think only about your own affairs, but be interested in others"—you will discover happiness in your home. Your attitude should never be that it is your partner's responsibility to make you happy. You must initially recognize your responsibility to make your partner happy.

There is an irrelevant and erroneous saying about marriage that has been around since Bev and I got married: *Marriage is a fifty-fifty proposition. You do your half, and I'll do mine.* Nothing could be further from the truth! Marriage, under God, should be a 100-percent-to-nothing proposition. That is, you should go into your marriage with the idea that you shall give all of yourself for the purpose of making your partner happy, expecting nothing in return. The result will be your own happiness.

A sharp young couple once came to see me with conflict written all over their faces. Travis had come from a very secure home. His greatest pleasure was to play in golf tournaments on weekends.

Tina came from a very insecure home where her parents' slash-and-burn marriage produced for Tina a desire to get away from it all. After four years of marriage, Travis and Tina had discovered that they were at such cross purposes that they knew their marriage would be over if they didn't do something. All was not lost, however. They both told me that they loved each other and wanted to get back on track.

I asked a series of questions, which helped me discover why they were both disappointed with the results of their marriage. Bottom line: They each came to the wedding with entirely different concepts of what it meant to be "married." Tina, who desired an escape from a suffocating home life, wanted marriage to be a blissful time of relaxation and family life, particularly on weekends. Travis saw marriage through a different prism: He thought marriage should be a relaxed home life five nights a week, followed by stimulating golf competition on the weekends that involved following a white ball around a verdant and manicured golf course. Friday, Saturday, and Sunday nights were reserved for spending time with Tina *and* friends.

Strangely enough, they both knew what the problem was; they just had never faced it before. Every time Travis entered another golf tournament, Tina would blow up and let loose a stream of cutting remarks. Then she would crawl into her self-protective shell of silence and frigidity, which only made matters worse. Travis felt guilty blowing off an entire Saturday—and some Sunday afternoons—shooting for the flag and trying to two-putt. Trying to do something social with Tina on Saturday night didn't calm the roiling waters.

Fortunately, these two people were mature enough to face the fact that their marriage was more important than "togetherness" or eighteen holes of golf. We worked out an agreement in which they would both give in to the other's desires on this matter. Travis cut back his golf to two weekends a month, and Tina promised that she would do something "active" with Travis on the weekends—instead of staying home and doing nothing.

Then one day a friend invited them to go waterskiing. Travis looked at his tournament calendar; this was one of the weekends that he said he would keep open. Because they both loved the water and the summer temperature was in the triple digits, Travis and Tina eagerly agreed to go. They discovered that they liked the boating lifestyle (cruising along the water and enjoying the good food that everyone packed and brought along) and waterskiing (shooting across a sheet of water at breakneck speed with the athletic grace needed to complete turns inside the buoys). After a few weekends of boating with their friends, Travis saw that doing something *with* Tina was far better for his marriage than playing best-ball tournaments with his buddies on the weekends.

Selfishness Is Universal

Selfishness, the single greatest enemy to a happy marriage, is a basic part of our fallen nature. All temperaments have one thing in common: the weakness of selfishness. This selfishness is revealed differently in each temperament. For example, the strong extrovert—Mr. or Mrs. Sanguine—reveals selfishness in egotism and angry impatience toward others. The moderate extrovert—Mr. or Mrs. Choleric—exhibits selfishness in an angry and cruel disregard for the feelings of others. Mr. or Mrs. Melancholy displays selfishness through self-centered introspection that produces fear and indecision. The quiet and easygoing Mr. or Mrs. Phlegmatic reveals selfishness by stubbornly refusing to get involved with the problems of others. Consequently, a phlegmatic person usually is fearful and doesn't want to get hurt.

The important thing to remember is that something can be done to overcome selfishness. The Bible tells us in 2 Corinthians 5:17, "What this means is that those who become Christians become new persons. They are not the same anymore, for the old life is gone. A new life has begun!" The Greek construction of this verse indicates the gradual passing away of old things, which includes one's natural selfishness. When Jesus Christ comes to live in a person's life, he creates a new nature that, if yielded to and nurtured, will overpower the old nature.

How to Overcome Selfishness

Selfishness can be corrected by the power of God in conjunction with a cooperative individual. God will give you the power—if you are willing to cooperate with him. The following steps are highly successful in changing selfish behavior into unselfish acts of thoughtfulness toward others.

* **Face your selfishness as a sin.** Until you can recognize your selfishness as a sin displeasing to God and to others, you will never be able to think of others before you think of yourself. Too many people make excuses like "I was raised that way," or "My parents were hippies, so they let me do whatever I wanted when I was growing up." The fact that your parents indulged you by not putting any limits on your behavior is no reason to perpetuate that mistake for the rest of your married life. Instead, face it as sin.

* **Don't try to hide behind academic or economic success to cover your selfishness.** Maturity is relative. That is, a man may be a brilliant scientist or an effective account manager, but he may act like an overgrown baby at home. A woman may be an effective organizer who keeps a department

working like a Swiss timepiece, but she may act like a childish and miserable wife at home. Face the truth that no matter who you are in the business or academic world, if you fail in your marriage, you have failed in an important area of your life. Selfishness is the greatest cause of marital failure.

Once you have faced the fact that your selfishness, despite how your partner acts toward you, is a sin before God, then you have taken a giant step. Think of it like a medical operation: Before you will submit to going under the knife, your doctor must convince you that you have a disease or some other physical malady. Excusing the symptoms will never correct the problem. The same principle applies in the emotional realm. As long as you cover up your selfishness by excusing or ignoring it, you will never act selflessly. Happy are those who understand that they, and they alone before God, are responsible for their actions and reactions.

* **Confess your selfishness as a sin.** There are no big sins or little sins in God's sight. Sin is sin. Whenever you act selfishly, be sufficiently objective about yourself to confess your sin to your heavenly Father, and then be assured that he will forgive you (1 John 1:9).

* **Ask God to take away the habit of being selfish.** "And we can be confident that he will listen to us whenever we ask him for anything in line with his will. And if we know he is listening when we make our requests, we can be sure that he will give us what we ask for" (1 John 5:14-15). Because it is not God's will that we act like selfish creatures, he will direct us in changing our habit of behaving selfishly.

* **Repair the damage done by your selfishness.** Some people cannot humble themselves enough to say, "I was wrong.

Will you forgive me?" They find it difficult to give up selfish behavior and to apologize after having acted selfishly. Apologize to whoever was hurt by your immaturity or self-seeking behavior, and watch what happens!

* **Repeat this formula every time you do or say something under the motivation of selfishness.** Keep this goal in mind: You want to become a happy, well-adjusted, and unselfish person whose company other people enjoy. In addition, your maturity may gradually inspire maturity in your partner. Before you realize it, the key of maturity will open many doors to happiness in your marriage.

KEY #2: MUTUAL SUBMISSION

No car—including the VW Beetle—can be driven by more than one person at a time. No corporation can function properly if it has two CEOs. This concept applies to married life as well. Couples need to mutually submit to each other, but at the end of the day, the husband must be the leader in the home.

It dismays me that this concept of male leadership has become so controversial since I wrote *How to Be Happy Though Married* back in the 1960s. Modern psychology and the media elite have turned *submission* into a loaded word that conjures up images of a ranting husband who browbeats his wife into doing things his way around the house and in the relationship. Nothing could be farther from the truth. What the Bible has to say on the subject doesn't give men license to lord over their wives. I believe what the Bible says is that God directs husbands to provide leadership in the home, but it must be done with a servant's attitude like the one Christ demonstrates to the church.

Let me jump-start this discussion by asking a set of questions:

What do you think *submission* means? Do you think society is better off today with the downgrading of the husband's role in the home? Do you think today's guys make good marriage material? (One thing I hear a lot of complaints about from single Christian women these days is the paucity of good Christian men suitable for marriage.) I'm convinced that God intended for a man to be the head of his home. If he is not, he will not have a sense of responsibility but will subconsciously feel he is married to a second mother. His children will soon detect who is boss, and when they grow to be teenagers, they will lose the natural respect for their father that is necessary for their adjustment to life.

Usually a wife-dominated home (or one where the husband has abdicated his leadership role) is a quarrelsome home. After a while, the husband tires of the fighting and crawls into his shell of introversion. The sad thing is that his wife will eventually grow to despise the person she dominates.

A Command of God

Let's review what the Bible says about this issue of mutual submission:

> *You will submit to one another out of reverence for Christ. You wives will submit to your husbands as you do to the Lord. For a husband is the head of his wife as Christ is the head of his body, the church; he gave his life to be her Savior. As the church submits to Christ, so you wives must submit to your husbands in everything.* EPHESIANS 5:21-24

> *So again I say, each man must love his wife as he loves himself, and the wife must respect her husband.* EPHESIANS 5:33

If you want to stir up a hornet's nest, then offer to teach a Sunday school class on mutual submission. I remember when I taught a Bible class on this topic before forty-five adults—twenty-three women and twenty-two men. I didn't hold anything back; I presented the results of the curse of Genesis 3 on the man, the woman, the ground, and the serpent. Concerning the woman, I pointed out that she had two parts to her curse: 1) pain in childbirth, and 2) being ruled over by her husband.

The next week I handed out a multiple-choice quiz, and one of the questions was this: *What was the result of the curse on the woman?* I received twenty-three female answers: She will have pain in childbirth. The twenty-two men answered: She shall be ruled over by her husband. A few of the men also included that she would have pain in childbirth. The fact that not one of those twenty-three women, who attended that Bible class for spiritual growth, had remembered the submission part of the curse illustrated to me how difficult it is for society to accept this concept.

God's Tool for Your Happiness

God never commands people to do something that is impossible or is not for their good. The Holy Spirit asks us in Romans 8:32, "Since God did not spare even his own Son but gave him up for us all, won't God, who gave us Christ, also give us everything else?" The answer to that is yes, because if God loved us so much that he gave his Son to die for us, he will certainly give us all those things that are for our good. Therefore, by faith accept the fact that submission to her husband is for a woman's good.

Let me add to this point. I have noticed from my counseling sessions with families that somewhere between the ages of thirty-five and forty-five, sometimes a woman will become what I call a "leaner." This means that she wants to be married to a man

that she can depend upon to be there through the tough times—
and tough times will happen during a marriage. The problem is
that if she has been aggressive in the early years of marriage and
has dominated her husband, she has taught him to lean on her.
When the tables are turned and she reaches the age where she
wants a man she can lean on, she finds that she has created a
leaner—not someone she can lean on. I've seen women at this
stage come to loathe the man whom they, in their younger years,
trained to be a docile, submissive spouse.

It is safe to assume that dominating wives have caused great
misery in marriage, both to themselves and to their partners. The
woman who enjoys bossing her husband when she is twenty-five
may find life turning into a nightmare as she advances in age. It is
an act of faith in a Christian woman's heart to assume that it is
essential that she be obedient to God and put herself in submission to her husband.

Subjection Is Not Slavery

When a Christian woman seeks God's grace and the filling of the
Holy Spirit to enable her to live in submission to her husband,
she is not in danger of becoming a slave. Frequently I have seen
women who have decided to become submissive find that the
reaction in their husband has been one of thoughtfulness and
kindness—and a cessation of hostilities between them. Usually a
woman finds that she fares far better when she accepts the submissive role than when she dominates.

Subjection does not mean that a woman can't voice her opinion by speaking "the truth in love" (Ephesians 4:15). Instead, she
should seek to be submissive to her husband's desires when he
reaches a decision, and then she should comply as much as is
humanly possible. There may be times when she will have to do

something that she really doesn't want to do, but by sowing the seeds of obedience on that matter, she will reap the harvest of blessing on many others. Always remember, you reap far more than you sow. If you sow submission in obedience to God, you will reap blessing in abundance; if you sow rebellion in disobedience to the will of God, you will reap abundant misery. I know that some women have a more aggressive temperament than their husbands, which makes it admittedly more difficult for them to be in submission. In fact, the only way I know they can submit is by recognizing that it is a spiritual responsibility. When this fact has been established in a woman's mind, she can summon the grace of God to be the submissive person God wants her to be.

Some years ago I counseled with a woman who was far more aggressive than her husband and found out through the years that she could have the final say-so regarding major decisions of the family. In temperament terms, he was an easygoing phlegmatic person, and she was a combination of the sanguine and choleric temperaments. Thus, when children came in to ask whether they could spend the night with friends or something like that, he would listen quietly and pause to reflect, wanting time to think over their request. When the children approached their mother, she made snap decisions and answered quickly.

When she reached her midthirties, she recognized that her husband was becoming Johnny Wallflower, a man who receded into a shell of compliance whenever she assumed dictatorial powers. When she became convinced of her need to submit to her husband for the Lord's sake, however, she asked God to help her bite her tongue and stifle her instinctive inclination to make spontaneous decisions. She decided to try to wait for her husband to make the decision.

She was amazed to find that, in a brief time, he gradually

assumed the decision-making responsibilities in the home. What was interesting to me, as I counseled with this woman, was the fact that the more she submitted, the more he led; the more he led, the happier he *and* she were. Their marriage gradually changed from the point of "married singles" to a union that sparked with genuine love and respect for each other. To me, this couple is a living example that a wife's submission to her husband is a key to a happy marriage.

Now that we've discussed the woman's role in submission, let's turn our focus to the man and his role in this submission process. A man who loves his wife as he loves himself (and men are in love with themselves, for you female readers) has the ability to achieve emotional oneness with his wife.

Fred Stoeker, who teaches premarriage classes at his church in Des Moines, Iowa, uses the illustration of the common candy cane to help young couples visualize this submission concept. "God says that the husband and wife shall be 'one flesh,'" says Fred. "Now envision the groom as a solid red candy cane and the bride as a solid white candy cane. Through marriage, these two canes become woven into a single candy cane. The colors of both the husband and wife, though distinct, now intertwine and are expressed together. In this striped candy cane we clearly visualize the role of male submission in marriage. The husband is the head. His red is the dominant color, but he must make the room for her white essence to play its part in the beauty of their marriage. The role of male submission is to yield his rights as the dominant color so that her gifts and essence might be expressed in one distinctive beauty. The role of female submission is to allow the husband the discretion to place the red stripes on the cane, but he must also allow the white to take its place with equal honor. This is where 'loving her as he loves himself' comes in. He must love white and make room for white as much as he loves red and makes room for red."

Men, are you yielding to honor her personal convictions and her soul essence? If so, you are practicing the role of mutual submission in a marriage.

KEY #3: LOVE

The third key that guarantees a happy marriage is love, yet probably no other word is more misunderstood in the English language than this four-letter one. Most people today do not know what love is, and today's Hollywood movies only muddy the waters. No wonder today's young people confuse love with physical attraction, sexual longings, personal desires, expressions of sympathy, or heartfelt compassion. Love may be one of the most common experiences known to men and women, but it is also one of the most difficult to define. A good place to start is with Webster's dictionary, which defines love as "a feeling of strong personal attachment induced by sympathetic understanding or by ties of kinship; ardent affection."

The Bible says the love of a husband for his wife should equal his love for himself. God instructed him to love his wife sacrificially as Christ loved and gave himself for the church. No woman can be unhappy when given that kind of love, and the husband that gives that kind of love will in turn be the recipient of sacrificial love.

Like God, love cannot be seen, but we know of its existence because of its effects. It is easier to describe love than to define it. Although many have attempted a description of love, in all the annals of literature none compares with those masterful words penned by the apostle Paul in the great love chapter, 1 Corinthians 13:

*Love is patient and kind. Love is not jealous or boastful or proud or
rude. Love does not demand its own way. Love is not irritable, and
it keeps no record of when it has been wronged. It is never glad
about injustice but rejoices whenever the truth wins out. Love
never gives up, never loses faith, is always hopeful, and endures
through every circumstance. (verses 4-7)*

Henry Drummond, in a book entitled *The Greatest Thing in the
World*, points out the nine characteristics of love found in the
preceding passage: patience, kindness, generosity, humility, courtesy, unselfishness, good temper, guilelessness, and sincerity.
Study these characteristics and examine your love to see whether
it meets God's standards of acceptable expression.

These nine characteristics or expressions of love communicate the love of one human being for another in terms meaningful to everyone, regardless of background. No one will naturally
express his or her love in all these characteristics. Some people
are patient and kind by nature, but they lack humility, generosity,
or confidence. Others are naturally sincere and courteous, but
they lack a good temper and are prone to be impatient. We all
need the power of the Holy Spirit to supply the kind of love that
God expects us to extend to our partners. The Holy Spirit gives
the Christian the ability to express complete love (Galatians
5:22-23).

The love that God requires of a husband for his wife and a wife
for her husband is admittedly a supernatural love. It is just not
possible for a man to love this way of his own accord. However,
since God never commands us to do that which he will not enable
us to do, we can call upon him, the author of love, and know that
he will supply us with this kind of supernatural love. The Bible tells
us, "But if we are living in the light of God's presence, just as Christ

is, then we have fellowship with each other, and the blood of Jesus, his Son, cleanses us from every sin" (1 John 1:7).

Both husband and wife are commanded to love each other, but it should be pointed out that while the wife is commanded once to love her husband (Titus 2:4), the husband is commanded at least three times to love his wife (Ephesians 5:25, 28, 33). There are two possible reasons for this: 1) women by nature have a greater capacity for love, and 2) men are knuckleheads who need to be reminded three times before something sinks in.

Love Is Kind

One of the primary characteristics of love is kindness. Somehow, many of those having trouble in marriage have forgotten to show kindness. They want to receive it, but they forget to give it. I remember the time that a warring couple who had been married for two years came in to see me. They were on the verge of separation, but they were fulfilling a promise that I required of all young couples in premarital class that if they were considering separation, before they called it quits, they would come and talk the matter over with me. Once they sat down in my office, I heard nothing but caustic and sarcastic remarks hurled across the room. The air was ugly.

After letting them vent their frustrations about the marriage, I gave the young couple the assignment of memorizing the nine characteristics of love and, since kindness to each other was conspicuously absent, I asked them to give their conversation "the kindness check." That is, every time they said something to each other they were to ask themselves, "Was that kind?" If not, they were to apologize and seek God's grace to be kind in their words to each other. Obviously, they found this directive to be near impossible for the first few days, but within two months this couple had reoriented themselves to the point that they could speak in relative kindness to each other. The result was a renewing of their genuine affection for each other.

Love Shows Approval

Most psychologists agree that everyone's basic needs are love and approval. The more we love a person, the more we naturally seek approval. For that reason, if someone does not express love by showing approval occasionally, he or she will live with a dissatisfied mate.

A man and woman came to see me one time who were complete opposites physically. The man was six-foot-four and weighed at least 235 pounds—a real linebacker type. The demure woman could not have weighed over 105 pounds and was a lithe and trim five feet tall. During counseling, things became heated. Joe Linebacker said in an emotion-packed voice, "Pastor, I haven't hit that woman in all the years we have been married," and as he said it he doubled up his gigantic fist. When I looked in Patty Demure's direction to gauge her reaction, I noticed tears running down her cheeks. "That is true," she said dejectedly, "but many times I wish he had hit me instead of clubbing me with disapproval!"

I honestly believe that disapproval inflicts more punishment upon another human being than physical abuse. The sad part is, the things people disapprove of in their partner are usually blown out of proportion, making the problems seem greater than they are. A high percentage of men would have to admit that he has a good wife, and the things that aggravate him comprise only 10 to 15 percent of the total person. His problem is that he has concentrated too much on the negative instead of thanking God for the positive.

It is good to ask yourself frequently, "Do I express approval of my partner?" That approval should be expressed both publicly, to assure your friends that you love your partner, and privately. Many people would have happier marriages and more responsive spouses if they commended their spouses for their accomplishments rather than expressing constant disapproval. Be sure of one thing: Your partner needs your approval for his or her adjustment in life and marriage. Most people respond better to commendation than to condemnation.

Love Can Be Rekindled

"I just don't love my husband anymore!" complained a young woman whose husband was not a Christian. She was looking for an escape hatch—divorce. She was unaware that not loving her husband did not necessarily testify to his unloveliness, but it did reveal her own lack of love. If you seek it, God will give you love for your partner, but if you need more prodding, then know that God has *commanded* you to love him or her. He will give you a new love for your partner, and it's all there for the asking.

You may be inclined to ask, "But is it worth it?" or "What if my partner doesn't deserve it?" That has nothing to do with your situation. You should love your partner for the Lord's sake. In addition, the principle of reaping what you sow means that loving will bring you love. If you go to God in faith and ask for his supply of love to give to your partner, then God's divine law will bring love to you.

The young woman previously mentioned prayed with me for that kind of love, and God gave it to her. After a month had passed, she said, "You just wouldn't believe the way God has returned my love for my husband! In fact, my husband has never been more loving and considerate in the eight years we have been married."

Women Respond to Love

I never cease to marvel at the endurance of a woman's love. Women have told me things about their husbands that could earn their husbands the title of "Biggest Jerk Alive," yet these women end by saying, "I still love the guy." Conversely, men would never put up with some of the things that most women are forced to endure. I suspect that is a carryover of a mother's love, which we tend to think of as the greatest illustration of human affection. Whatever the cause, I am convinced that a woman has a far greater capacity to love a man than a man has to love a woman. I have yet to meet a woman who will not respond to love.

I make this observation with some hesitation since no man in his right mind would present himself as an authority on women. We can agree that women are "complex creatures." After counseling several thousand women over fifty years, I have arrived at one basic conclusion: Most men do not know how to make a woman happy. I have learned that it isn't money, diamonds, furs, houses, or other things that make a woman happy, but just plain love. Not lovemaking alone, but the treatment that produces lovemaking—kindness, thoughtfulness, understanding, acceptance or approval, and the recognition from the husband that he is just not complete without her.

Happy is the wife whose husband knows and tells her that if given the chance to marry all over again, he would still choose her. Whenever a man tells me, "My wife doesn't love me anymore," I immediately know that he has not loved his wife "as his own body." If he had, she would return his love—that's just the nature of women.

KEY #4: COMMUNICATION

Young lovers rarely have a communication problem. They love to talk and talk long into the night about anything. Somehow, that ability often vanishes after they are married. Lack of communication is almost always a problem for the couples who come to me for marriage counseling. If truth be told, however, it's not lack of communication, it's *wrong* communication. Communicating under the pressure of anger and shouting at the top of one's voice is the wrong approach. This is communication that could well be omitted in every marriage. Problems and differences in a marriage are not dangerous; it's the inability to communicate about those differences, or problem areas, that is dangerous. As long as two people can keep the lines of communication open and can freely express their feelings, differences can be resolved.

The following statement by Ann Landers in her syndicated column illustrates the importance of communication:

The most important single ingredient in a marriage is the ability to communicate. If my mail is a fair reflection of what goes on with Mr. and Mrs. America behind closed doors (and I think it is), most marital problems stem from the inability of two people to talk to each other. How precious is the ability to communicate! The mature man and woman recognize that there is unity in love, but simultaneously there must be freedom for both individuals. Neither should be swallowed up by the other. Each must maintain his personality and his identity. A sound marriage should mean togetherness, but it also should mean respect for the rights and privileges of the other party. The couples who are secure in marriage can be honest about all kinds of feelings. The man and woman who can air their differences, get the hostility out of their system, then kiss and make up have an excellent chance of growing old together.

It has been amazing to me to find that many couples settle for a second-rate marriage relationship primarily because they have never learned to communicate. I remember the time when a woman, who did not know I had already talked with her husband, came to me for counseling. Their problem seemed to be that the woman was not completely committed to the Lord. But her lack of commitment to Christ was not the real problem. A few weeks later she gave me a ride home after a meeting and spontaneously invited me in to talk to both of them. Her husband was surprised, but he quickly responded. Suddenly I was acting as a referee between two friends.

For twenty minutes she calmly mentioned some of her pet gripes and objections to her husband. None of them were unusual or severe, but when added together, they created a spirit of resentment in her. Some things went back to within six months after they were married. When she finished, he very calmly said to her, "Honey, why in the world didn't you tell me these things years ago?" (They had been married ten years.) Her answer was, "I was afraid to. I thought you would explode."

Knowing that every argument has two sides, I asked the husband if he would like to voice any objections to her as kindly as he could. For a similar time, he rehearsed her weaknesses and when he finished, she turned and said, "Why didn't you tell me this before?" He replied, "Because I thought you would get mad and go into a long period of silence." By learning to communicate, that couple soon learned to exchange their honest feelings without fear. The happy ending occurred when the wife could fully commit herself to Christ.

Communication Killers

How does the wall of resistance to communication gradually build up between two people who love each other? Naturally, neither plans to build such a wall; it gradually grows from the time of their first breakdown in communication. Dr. Henry Brandt, my mentor, once shared with a group of ministers the three weapons that people use to defend themselves. As you look at these three weapons, you will find that married people use them to gradually build a wall of resistance so they are no longer able to communicate.

1. The first weapon is explosion. Whenever people are told about their shortcomings, rather than face them honestly, their natural reaction is to explode. This explosion is the result of inner anger and hostility that cause them to attempt self-protection. Dr. Brandt pointed out that no nakedness is comparable to psychological nakedness. When someone, particularly our partner, points out our deficiencies, we tend to grasp for something to cover us; if we happen to be sanguine or choleric in temperament, we will tend to utilize anger and express it through explosion. What this does is teach your partner that "you can't come that close to my intimate weaknesses; if you do, I'll explode."

2. The second weapon is tears. This weapon is used mainly by women, though sometimes a melancholy or sanguine man will resort to it. Like the other weapons, it is a way of saying to your partner, "Don't tell me my shortcomings or I'll cry!" The first spat after marriage often leaves the bride in tears. This teaches the new husband that she has a breaking point, so subconsciously he will tend to hold back his communication lest he make her cry. Thus, another brick is laid in the wall that stifles communication.

A parenthetical note is appropriate here on feminine tears. Husbands, learn to distinguish between your wife's tears of emotion, stress, joy, and self-pity. Women are far more intricate creatures than men, and they often show their emotions through tears. Don't despise your wife's tears! Be patient and kind, for the emotional creature you married is just being a woman. In fact, I have found that the woman who is easily moved to tears has the greatest capacity to express her emotions in every area of life. Usually that type of wife is more responsive to tenderness and lovemaking than the dry-eyed woman. In fact, years ago I concluded that women who weep easily tend to act more loving, while tearless wives often find it difficult to express their emotions at all.

If your wife is emotionally expressive, thank God! Her tears testify to this emotional richness that makes her a compassionate mother and loving wife. Be particularly thoughtful during her menstrual period, as she may be unusually emotional then. A little TLC—tender loving care—during that time is like laying up treasure in heaven: it pays off by and by.

3. The third weapon is silence. Silence is a very dangerous tool because it rapidly stifles communication and takes a heavy toll physically and spiritually upon a person. It takes tremendous power to be silent for a long time; anger can supply that power.

As a way of illustration, some years ago I counseled with a couple who told me that one of their problems was that the man was slow of speech and his wife was just the opposite. Whenever he would try to express himself, she couldn't wait for him to finish. Instead, she butted in with her two cents' worth before he had even finished making his point. In fact, her constant interruptions often reminded me of a machine gun as she blasted away at him. He soon learned that he was no match for her when it came to verbal fisticuffs.

One day I met him at church and casually asked, "How are things going?"

"Wonderful," he replied. "I finally learned how to handle that woman!"

"How did you manage that?" I asked. I was genuinely interested in what his answer would be.

"Through silence. The one thing she can't stand is for me to be silent. When she crosses me, I will go for long periods without talk-ing. In fact, I even went five days one time without speaking to her."

"I don't think you're going to want to do that long term," I said. "That will be a very expensive tool because pent-up anger and bitterness produce ulcers." Little did I realize how prophetic my statement was, for in a matter of weeks I got the report that he had a bleeding ulcer. Anger is one of the leading causes of ulcers, high blood pressure, and several other diseases.

How much better it would be if two people would learn to communicate their differences freely, thereby avoiding not only problems but also side effects. Remember, all anger, bitterness, and wrath grieve the Holy Spirit (Ephesians 4:30-32). No husband or wife can walk in the Spirit and maintain anger toward his or her spouse (Galatians 5:16).

How to Communicate

The Bible teaches that we should speak "the truth in love" (Ephe-sians 4:15). One should bear in mind, however, that the more truth you speak, the more love you should use in conveying that truth, because truth is a sharp, two-edged sword. In other words, use it carefully. When you have an area in your marriage that needs communication, consider using the following steps in presenting your case.

* **Pray for the wisdom of God and the filling of the Holy Spirit.** When you seek God's wisdom, you may find that your objection to your partner's behavior is not really valid. Or you may sense the leading of the Spirit of God to go ahead and communicate your problem.
* **Plan a time that is good for your partner.** It's foolhardy to discuss anything of a serious or negative nature after 10:00

or 10:30 P.M. Life tends to look darker and problems loom larger at night. If your partner is not an early riser, however, the morning is not the best time either. Many couples find that after dinner is a good time for communication. If you have small children, then this is a less-than-desirable time, so maybe you should find a baby-sitter and go out for something to eat. The idea is to find a time when you are in the best possible mood to look objectively at yourselves.

* **Speak the truth in love—in kind words say exactly what is on your heart.** Make sure that your love is equal to your truth.

* **Don't lose your temper.** Wise couples determine early in their marriage that they will not raise their voices at each other. Under anger, we often say more than we intend to, and usually this excess is cutting, cruel, and unnecessary. Anger on one person's part usually precipitates an angry response by the other. Kindly state your objection in love, but state it only once; then trust the Holy Spirit to use your words in effecting a change.

* **Allow for reaction time.** Don't be surprised if your communication is met with an explosive reaction, particularly in the earliest stages of marriage. Remember, you have the advantage in that you know what you will say. Hopefully, you have prayed it over and have been able to prepare yourself, but your partner will probably be taken by surprise. Don't defend yourself, but let your partner think about what you have said. He or she may never admit that you are right, but usually you will find that it will create a change in behavior. After all, aren't you more interested in that than you are in verbal agreement?

* **Commit the problem to God.** Once you have told your partner, you have done about all you can do, humanly

speaking, to change their behavior. From that point on, you must trust God either to help your partner change any objectionable habits or to supply you with the necessary grace to live with those habits (2 Corinthians 12:9).

Two Golden Expressions

There are two golden expressions that every married person should communicate to his or her partner repeatedly throughout the marriage.

I'm sorry.

Everyone makes mistakes. Romans 3:23 points out that "all have sinned; all fall short of God's glorious standard." You will sin against your partner and your partner will sin against you repeatedly in a normal marriage. If, however, you are willing to face your mistakes and apologize to your companion, you will find that resistance dissolves and a spirit of forgiveness prevails. If you are unwilling to acknowledge your mistakes, then you have a serious spiritual problem—pride.

One time as I counseled with a couple the wife tearfully said, "My husband has never apologized to me in the twenty-three years we have been married."

Turning to him, I asked, "Is this true? Have you ever done anything wrong?"

"Oh, of course," he quickly replied. "I am only human."

"Then why have you never apologized?"

"I didn't think it was very manly for me to apologize," he explained. "My father never apologized to my mother."

Unfortunately, this man grew up with a father who made a very terrible decision never to apologize. This man was perpetuating that mistake and reaping the resultant misery. When you are wrong, face it objectively and honestly admit it—both to yourself and to your partner.

I love you.

These three simple words are the second golden expression in a marriage. I have already pointed out that it is absolutely necessary for every human being to be loved. Your partner will never tire of hearing you tell him or her of your love. This expression of love seems to be more meaningful to women than to men, but I am inclined to believe women are just more prone to admit their need for it, and that men need it also.

A man came in to see me the day after his wife of fifteen years had left him. He was a brilliant engineer with an I.Q. of 148, and he knocked down seventy-five thousand dollars a year. As he described the shipwreck of his marriage, he acknowledged that for the past ten years he had not told his wife that he loved her.

"Why is that?" I asked.

"Why should I have to tell her? I have demonstrated it faithfully for fifteen years."

"How did you manage that?"

"When she didn't like the house we lived in, I bought her another house. When she didn't like her car, I bought her another car. When she didn't like the carpeting, I had the old carpet taken out and replaced. If I didn't love her, how come we have five children?"

The amazing thing about the whole situation was that his wife had run off with a sailor who made two thousand dollars a month and looked enough like her husband to be his twin brother. In exasperation he asked me, "What could that poor sailor possibly give to my wife that I haven't already given her?"

"Just one thing," I replied. "Love."

As brilliant an engineer as he was, this man was an ignoramus as a husband. Their problem could have been solved if he had been willing to give of himself and let her know that he loved her and approved of her. He couldn't seem to understand that although saying "I love you" sounded childish to him, it was meaningful to her. Nor did he understand that if he had not been so selfish, he would have been more than willing to express in words what she wanted to hear. The more your partner loves you, the more he or she enjoys hearing you express your love. Say it meaningfully and say it often.

KEY #5: PRAYER

I already discussed prayer in chapter 3 ("Spiritual Adjustment"), so I will not enter into a lengthy explanation here. The six keys to a happy marriage would not be complete, however, if I did not include prayer. Prayer to your heavenly Father is the best means of communication between two people. Many a marriage has been completely transformed by initiating a practice of regular prayer. One method I heartily recommend is conversational prayer.

Bev and I have found praying together in our bed before we fall asleep to be a tremendous blessing. The success of our marriage for more than fifty years can be attributed to obeying Proverbs 3:5-6, which states, "Trust in the Lord with all your heart; do not depend on your own understanding. Seek his will in all you do, and he will direct your paths." We were taught early on to seek the Lord's guidance before making every major decision.

Not long ago, we were invited to make a trip to Israel, with all our expenses to be paid for by the state of Israel. Ten days before our departure, I had a bad feeling about it, probably because of the pressures of duties at home.

When we went to bed that night, I mentioned to Bev how I was having second thoughts about the trip. We both knew what came next: We clasped hands and each lifted up the situation to God in prayer, asking the Lord to give us a peace in our hearts about what we should do.

The next morning over breakfast, we raised the Israel trip issue again, and as we both discussed it, we concluded that we should cancel the trip. I did just that: I made a phone call and expressed our apologies in canceling the trip. Following that, Bev and I enjoyed the peace of God that passes all understanding (Philippians 4:7).

During the week we should have been in Israel, an emergency came up that demanded my presence at an important proceeding in the Los Angeles area. Then I read in the newspaper that a terrorist had set off a bomb in a Jerusalem shopping mall, killing six and injuring eleven. Would Bev and I have been passing through the mall at that fateful time? We will never know, but we know that praying about the matter together gave us the peace to know that we had done the right thing in canceling the trip. I can assure you that sharing burdens in prayer further strengthens the common bond that exists between a husband and wife.

One time I was counseling two different couples. I asked each couple to try this method of prayer before falling asleep. One couple started that very night, and within a week, they called to say they didn't feel they needed to come in for counseling anymore because "the Lord has solved our difficulties." The other couple refused to enter into this prayer relationship and continued living in a marriage that I would call an "armed truce."

Someone once said, "You can't quarrel with the woman you pray with every day." There is something humbling about getting down on your knees together or holding hands in bed that is emotionally beneficial to both parties. Many couples have

acknowledged that they rise from their knees more genuinely inter-
twined than before they prayed. Try it and see.

Who should initiate prayer? Ordinarily the husband, because
he's the head of the home, but if he doesn't, the wife can. The time
spent in prayer together can very well be the most valuable time of
your lives. Don't tarry until the complexities of life drive you to
your knees. If you wait to pray together until some difficulty arises,
you will find that when you need God most, you know him the
least. Learn to know him together in prayer now so that when life's
tidewaters rise up, you can go in prayer to the one you have
already learned to know as a close friend.

KEY #6: CHRIST

Things equal to the same thing are equal to each other is a
well-known mathematical principle, and it can be applied to
marriage. If two people are properly related in a personal way to
Jesus Christ, they will most likely be properly related to each other.
Jesus Christ wants to be Lord and Savior of you as an individual.
Then, he wants to be the Lord of your marriage. If he is, then the
home you are building will abide in lasting peace and blessing. If
he is not the spiritual head of your home, you will find that you
will never experience all the blessings that God has waiting for you
in marriage. Jesus said, "For apart from me you can do nothing"
(John 15:5).

If you have never received Jesus Christ, may I suggest that right
now you bow your head and invite him into your life. He said,
"Behold, I stand at the door and knock. If anyone hears My voice
and opens the door, I will come in to him and dine with him, and
he with Me" (Revelation 3:20, NKJV). If you desire him to come into
your life, all you need to do is ask him. Once inside, he then, by
his Spirit, will direct you in all areas of life.

The test of all marital behavior in relationship to Christ should be, "Is it done with his approval?" The Scripture teaches, "And whatever you do or say, let it be as a representative of the Lord Jesus, all the while giving thanks through him to God the Father" (Colossians 3:17). Jesus Christ is interested in every area of your life: physical, emotional, financial, and spiritual. Living in accordance with his will, as revealed in his Word, is the most important thing you can do to ensure a happy marriage. You can then say:

Christ is the head of this house,
The unseen guest at every meal,
The silent listener to every conversation.

Without a doubt, Christ is the greatest key to happiness in marriage. If you ask God to help you utilize these six keys in your life and marriage, your home will become increasingly blessed and happy.

I have seen many hopeless marriages take on new life and love when the couple received Jesus personally as Lord and Savior and recognized that he brings a dimension of love into a relationship that cannot be achieved on any other level.

THE SPIRIT-FILLED PERSON

THE ESSENTIAL THING in the life of any Christian is to be filled with the Holy Spirit![1] The Lord Jesus said, "For apart from me you can do nothing" (John 15:5). Christ is in believers in the person of his Holy Spirit. Therefore, if we are filled with his Spirit, he works fruitfully through us. If we are not filled with the Holy Spirit, we are unproductive.

It is almost impossible to exaggerate how dependent we are upon the Holy Spirit. We are dependent on him for convicting us of sin before and after our salvation, for giving us understanding of the gospel, for causing us to be born again, for empowering us to witness, for guiding us in our prayer life—in fact, for everything. It is no wonder that evil spirits have tried to counterfeit and confuse the work of the Holy Spirit.

There is probably no subject in the Bible that generates more confusion today than that of being filled with the Holy Spirit. Satan, for his part, places two obstacles before us: (1) he tries to keep us from receiving Christ as Savior in the first place, and (2) if he fails in this, he then tries to keep us from understanding the

[1]This appendix is a chapter from Tim LaHaye's book *Spirit-Controlled Temperament*.

importance and the work of the Holy Spirit. Once you are converted, however, Satan takes a different tack. He tries to get you to associate the filling of the Holy Spirit with emotional excesses, or, the opposite swing of the pendulum, to ignore the Holy Spirit altogether.

One of the false impressions gained from people and not from the Word of God is that there is some special "feeling" when one is filled with the Holy Spirit. Before we examine how to be filled with the Holy Spirit, let us find out what the Bible says we can expect when we are filled with the Holy Spirit.

What to Expect When Filled with the Holy Spirit

1. The nine temperament traits of the Spirit-filled life as found in Galatians 5:22-23 are love, joy, peace, patience, kindness, goodness, faithfulness, gentleness, and self-control.

   Any individual who is filled with the Holy Spirit will manifest these characteristics! You don't have to try to be filled, or play a part, or act out a role: You will just be this way when the Spirit has control of your nature.

   Many who claim to have had the "filling" or, as some call it, "the anointing" know nothing of love, joy, peace, patience, kindness, goodness, faithfulness, gentleness, and self-control. These attributes are, however, the hallmark of the person filled with the Holy Spirit.

2. A joyful, thanks-giving heart and a submissive spirit.

   When the Holy Spirit fills your life, the Bible says he will cause you to have a singing, thanks-giving heart and a submissive spirit.

   Don't be drunk with wine, because that will ruin your life. Instead, let the Holy Spirit fill and control you. Then you

will sing psalms and hymns and spiritual songs among your-
selves, making music to the Lord in your hearts. And you
will always give thanks for everything to God the Father in
the name of our Lord Jesus Christ. And further, you will
submit to one another out of reverence for Christ.
EPHESIANS 5:18-21

The Spirit of God can change a gloomy or griping heart
into a song-filled, thankful heart. He is also able to solve
your rebellious nature by increasing your faith to the point
that you really believe the best way to live is in submission
to the will of God.

The same three results of the Spirit-filled life are also the
results of the Word-filled life, as found in Colossians 3:16-19.

Let the words of Christ, in all their richness, live in your
hearts and make you wise. Use his words to teach and coun-
sel each other. Sing psalms and hymns and spiritual songs
to God with thankful hearts. And whatever you do or say, let
it be as a representative of the Lord Jesus, all the while
giving thanks through him to God the Father. You wives
must submit to your husbands, as is fitting for those who
belong to the Lord.

It's no accident that we find the results of the Spirit-filled
life (Ephesians 5:18-21) and those of the Word-filled life to
be one and the same. The Lord Jesus said that the Holy
Spirit is "the Spirit of truth" (John 14:17, NKJV), and he also
said of the Word of God, "Your word is truth" (John 17:17,
NKJV).

It is easy to understand why the Word-filled life causes
the same results as the Spirit-filled life, for the Holy Spirit is

the author of the Word of God. This highlights the error of those who try to receive the Holy Spirit through a once-for-all experience rather than an intimate relationship with God, which Jesus described as "abiding in me."

This relationship is possible in the Christian's life as God communes with him and fills his life through the "word of truth" and as he communes with God in prayer, guided by the "Spirit of truth." The conclusion that we can clearly draw here is that the Christian who is Spirit-filled will be Word-filled, and the Word-filled Christian who obeys the Spirit will be Spirit-filled.

3. The Holy Spirit gives us power to witness (Acts 1:8).

> *But when the Holy Spirit has come upon you, you will receive power and will tell people about me everywhere— in Jerusalem, throughout Judea, in Samaria, and to the ends of the earth.*

The Lord Jesus told his disciples, "It is actually best for you that I go away, because if I don't, the Counselor [the Holy Spirit] won't come" (John 16:7). That explains why the last thing Jesus did before he ascended into heaven was to tell his disciples that the Holy Spirit would come upon them and change their lives.

Although the disciples had spent three years with Jesus personally, had heard his messages several times, and were the best-trained witnesses he had, he still instructed them not to leave Jerusalem "until the Father sends you what he promised" (Acts 1:4). All of their training obviously was incapable of producing fruit of itself without the power of the Holy Spirit. It is well known that when the Holy Spirit came on the day of Pentecost, they witnessed his power and saw three thousand persons saved.

We, too, can expect to have power to witness when filled with the Holy Spirit. That power is not always discernible, but it must be accepted by faith. When we have met the conditions for the filling of the Holy Spirit, we should be careful to believe that we have witnessed in the power of the Spirit, whether or not we see the results. Because the Holy Spirit demonstrated his presence on the day of Pentecost so dramatically—and because occasionally we see the evidence of the Holy Spirit in our life—we come to think that it should always be obvious, but that is not true.

It is possible to witness in the power of the Holy Spirit and still not see an individual come to a saving knowledge of Christ. For in the sovereign plan of God, he has chosen never to violate our freedom of choice. Therefore, individuals can be witnessed to in the power of the Holy Spirit and still reject the Savior. You may then go away with the erroneous idea that you were unsuccessful, but you cannot always equate success in witnessing with the power to witness!

Years ago it was my privilege to witness to an eighty-year-old man. Because of his age, I made a special effort to meet the conditions of being filled with the Holy Spirit before I went to his home. He paid very close attention when I presented the gospel by using the "four spiritual laws." When I finished and asked whether he would like to receive Christ right then, he said, "No, I'm not ready yet." I persisted without pushing, but he was adamant. I left that night amazed that a man eighty years of age could say that he was "not ready yet." I concluded that I had not witnessed in the power of the Holy Spirit.

A short time later I returned to see the man and found that he had passed his eighty-first birthday. Once again I started to present the gospel to him, but he informed me that he had already received Christ. When I asked him for details, he told me that he had studied the "four spiritual laws" that I had written out on a sheet of paper. Then, alone in his room, he got down on his knees and invited Christ Jesus into his life as Savior and Lord. Afterward, I wondered how many other times in my life, because I had not seen an immediate response to the gospel, I had wrongly concluded that the Spirit had not filled me with his power to witness.

To be sure, a Christian life, when filled with the Holy Spirit, will produce fruit. For if you examine what Jesus meant when he said, "Remain in me" (John 15) and what the Bible teaches in relationship to being filled with the Spirit, you will find that they are one and the same experience.

Jesus said, "Those who remain in me, and I in them, will produce much fruit" (John 15:5). Therefore, we can conclude that the abiding life or the Spirit-filled life will produce fruit. But it is wrong to require every witnessing opportunity to demonstrate whether we are empowered by the Spirit to witness. Instead, we must meet the conditions for the filling of the Holy Spirit and then believe—not by results or sight or feeling but by faith—that we are filled.

4. The Holy Spirit will glorify Jesus Christ (John 16:13-14).

> *When the Spirit of truth comes, he will guide you into all truth. He will not be presenting his own ideas; he will be telling you what he has heard. He will tell you about the*

future. He will bring me glory by revealing to you whatever he receives from me.

A fundamental principle should always be kept in mind regarding the work of the Holy Spirit: He does not glorify himself but the Lord Jesus Christ. Anytime anyone but the Lord Jesus receives the glory, you can be sure that what is done is not done in the power of or under the direction of the Holy Spirit, for his express work is to glorify Jesus. This test should always be given to any work that claims to be the work of God's Holy Spirit.

The late F. B. Meyer told the story of a woman missionary who came to him at a Bible conference after he had spoken on the subject of how to be filled with the Holy Spirit. She confessed that she was never consciously filled with the Holy Spirit and was going to go up to the prayer chapel to spend the day in soul-searching. She wanted to know whether she could receive the Holy Spirit's filling.

Late that evening she came back just as Dr. Meyer was leaving the auditorium. "How was it, sister?" he asked.

"I'm not quite sure," she replied.

"What did you do?"

She explained her day's activities of reading the Word, praying, confessing her sins, and asking for the filling of the Holy Spirit. Then she stated, "I do not feel filled with the Holy Spirit."

"Tell me, sister, how is it between you and the Lord Jesus?"

Her face lit up, and with a smile she said, "Oh, Dr. Meyer, I have never had a more blessed time of fellowship with the Lord Jesus in all of my life."

"Sister, that is the Holy Spirit!" said Dr. Meyer.

The Holy Spirit will always make the believer more conscious of the Lord Jesus than of himself.

Now, in review, let us summarize what we can expect when we are filled with the Holy Spirit. Very simply, it is the nine temperament characteristics of the Spirit; a singing, thanks-giving heart that gives us a submissive attitude; and the power to witness. These characteristics will glorify the Lord Jesus Christ.

But what about "feelings" or "ecstatic experiences"? The Bible does not tell us to expect these things when we are filled with the Holy Spirit; therefore, we should not expect that which the Bible does not promise.

How to Be Filled with the Holy Spirit

The filling of the Holy Spirit is not optional equipment in the Christian life but a command of God! Ephesians 5:18 tells us, "Don't be drunk with wine, because that will ruin your life. Instead, let the Holy Spirit fill and control you." This statement is in the imperative mood; therefore, we should accept it as a command.

God never makes it impossible for us to keep his commandments. So, obviously, if he commands us to be filled with the Holy Spirit, and he does, then it must be possible for us to be filled with his Spirit. I would like to give five simple steps for being filled with the Holy Spirit:

1. Undergo a period of self-examination. (Acts 20:28 and 1 Corinthians 11:28)

   If you are interested in the filling of the Holy Spirit, you must examine yourself, not to see whether you measure up to the standards of other people or the traditions and requirements of your church but to see if you exhibit the previously mentioned results of being filled with the Holy Spirit. If you do not find that you are glorifying Jesus, if you don't have power to witness, if you lack a joyful and submissive spirit, then your self-examination will reveal those areas in which you are deficient and will uncover the sin that causes them.

2. Confess all of your known sins to God.

First John 1:9 says that if we confess our sins, then God is faithful to forgive us our sins and to cleanse us from all unrighteousness. The Bible does not put an evaluation on one sin or another but seems to judge all sin alike.

After examining ourselves in the light of the Word of God, we should confess all sins brought to mind by the Holy Spirit, including those characteristics of the Spirit-filled life that we lack. Until we start calling our lack of compassion, our lack of self-control, our lack of humility, our wrath where there should be gentleness, our bitterness where there should be kindness, and our unbelief where there should be faith sins, we will never have the filling of the Holy Spirit.

The moment we recognize these deficiencies as sin and confess them to God, he will "cleanse us from all unrighteousness" (1 John 1:9, NKJV). Until we have done this, we cannot have the filling of the Holy Spirit, for he fills only clean vessels (2 Timothy 2:21, NKJV).

3. Be sure to submit yourself completely to God.

So you should consider yourselves dead to sin and able to live for the glory of God through Christ Jesus. Do not let sin control the way you live; do not give in to its lustful desires. Do not let any part of your body become a tool of wickedness, to be used for sinning. Instead, give yourselves completely to God since you have been given new life. And use your whole body as a tool to do what is right for the glory of God. ROMANS 6:11-13

To be filled with the Holy Spirit, you must make yourself completely available to God to do anything the Holy Spirit directs him to do. If there is anything in your life that you are unwilling to do or to be, then you are resisting God, and this always limits God's Spirit!

Do not make the mistake of being afraid to give yourself to God! Romans 8:32 tells us, "Since God did not spare even his own Son but gave him up for us all, won't God, who gave us Christ, also give us everything else?" It is clear from this verse that if God loved us so much as to give his Son to die for us, certainly he is interested in nothing but our good; therefore, we can trust him with our lives. You will never find any miserable Christians in the center of God's will, for they will always follow his directions with an appetite and desire to do his will.

Resisting the Lord through rebellion obviously stifles the filling of the Spirit. Israel limited the Lord, not only through unbelief but also, as Psalm 78:8 tells us, by becoming "stubborn, rebellious, and unfaithful, refusing to give their hearts to God." All resistance to the will of God will keep you from being filled with the Holy Spirit. For to be filled with his Spirit, we must yield ourselves to his Spirit just as someone yields himself or herself to wine for its filling.

Ephesians 5:18 says, "Don't be drunk with wine,

because that will ruin your life. Instead, let the Holy Spirit fill and control you." When you're drunk, you are controlled by alcohol—you live, act, and are dominated by its influence. So with the filling of the Holy Spirit, your actions must be dominated by and dictated by the Holy Spirit. For consecrated Christians, this is often the most difficult thing to do, for we can always find some worthy purpose for our life, not realizing that we are often filled with ourselves rather than with the Holy Spirit as we seek to serve the Lord.

Years ago, while speaking at a high school and college camp, I heard a thrilling testimony from a ministerial student who said that for the first time he realized what it meant to be filled with the Holy Spirit. As far as he knew, he had not been guilty of the usual sins, although he admitted one area of resistance in his life. He loved to preach, and the possibilities of being a pastor or evangelist appealed to him very much, but he did not want the Lord to make a missionary out of him.

During that week the Holy Spirit spoke to the lad about that very vocation. The student wrestled with God, but then he submitted everything to the Lord and said, "Yes, I'll go to the ends of the earth." For the first time, he experienced the true filling of the Holy Spirit. Later he said, "I don't believe the Lord wants me to be a missionary after all; he just wanted me to be *willing* to be a missionary."

When you give your life to God, do not attach any strings or conditions to it. He is such a God of love that you can safely give yourself without reservation, knowing that his plan for and use of your life is far better than any plan you could make. And remember, an attitude of yielding everything to God is absolutely necessary for the filling of his

Spirit. Your will is the will of the flesh, and the Bible says that "the flesh profits nothing" (John 6:63, NKJV).

Yielding to God is sometimes difficult after you have solved the five big questions of life:

1. Where shall I attend college?
2. What career shall I pursue?
3. Whom shall I marry?
4. Where shall I live?
5. Where shall I attend church?

A Spirit-filled Christian will be sensitive to the Spirit's leading in small decisions as well as big ones. But it has been my observation that many Christians who have made the decisions on life's five big questions are still not filled with the Spirit.

Someone has suggested that being yielded to the Spirit is being available to the Spirit. Peter and John in Acts 3 make a good case for that interpretation. They were on their way to the temple to pray when they saw the lame man begging alms. Because they were sensitive to the Holy Spirit, they healed him "in the name of Jesus Christ of Nazareth" (Acts 3:6). The man began leaping about and praising God until a crowd gathered. Peter, still sensitive to the Holy Spirit, began preaching, and "many of the people who heard their message believed it, so that the number of believers totaled about five thousand men, not counting women and children" (Acts 4:4).

Frequently, I fear, we are so engrossed in some good Christian activity that we are not "available" when the Spirit leads. In my own life, I have found that when someone asks me to do some good thing and I give a negative response, it is the flesh rather than the Spirit that leads me. Many Christians have said no to the Holy Spirit when they were offered an opportunity to teach Sunday school, sing in the choir, or serve the Lord in some other capacity. Not every "open door of service" is the leading of the Holy Spirit, but it usually is an opportunity worth praying about.

Many a Christian says, "Lord, here I am, use me!" but when asked to do something for the church, replies that he or she is "too busy" to take on that responsibility. When you yield unto God "as being alive from the dead" (Romans 6:13, NKJV), you take time to do what the Spirit directs you to do.

4. Ask to be filled with the Holy Spirit.

If you sinful people know how to give good gifts to your children, how much more will your heavenly Father give the Holy Spirit to those who ask him. LUKE 11:13

When you have examined yourself, confessed all known sins, and yielded yourself without reservation to God, you are then ready to do the one thing you must do to receive the Spirit of God. Very simply, it is to ask to be filled with the Spirit. Any suggestion to wait or tarry or labor or suffer is someone else's suggestion. Only the disciples were told to wait, and that was because the day of Pentecost had not yet come. Since that day, God's children only have to ask for his filling to experience it.

The Lord Jesus compares this to our treatment of our earthly children. Certainly good parents would not make their children beg for something they wanted them to have. How much less would God make us beg for an experience of being filled with the Holy Spirit that he has commanded us to have? "Ask, and it will be given to you," Jesus said (Luke 11:9, NKJV). It's just as simple as that! But don't forget Step 5:

5. Believe you are filled with the Holy Spirit! And thank him for his filling.

> *Let not him who eats despise him who does not eat, and let not him who does not eat judge him who eats; for God has received him.* ROMANS 14:3, NKJV

> *No matter what happens, always be thankful, for this is God's will for you who belong to Christ Jesus.*
> 1 THESSALONIANS 5:18

If you have fulfilled the first four steps, then thank God for his filling by faith. Don't wait for feelings, don't wait for any physical signs, but fasten your faith to the Word of God that is independent of feeling. Feelings of assurance of the Spirit's filling often follow our taking God at his Word and believing he has filled us, but they neither cause the filling nor determine whether we are filled. Believing we are filled with the Spirit is merely taking God at his Word, and that is the only absolute this world has (Matthew 24:35).

FROM MY COUNSELING FILES

ONE OF THE GREATEST REWARDS when I was a pastor was to see the power of Jesus Christ transform a depressingly miserable marriage into a happy one. A pastor sees this transformation more graphically in the counseling room than anywhere else. Every minister has his own philosophy of counseling—and no one method is foolproof. The stories that follow are true, although the names and revealing details have been modified to avoid betraying confidences. I am convinced that true stories involving human beings in some way parallel the situations and happenings of others. Also, these episodes will help illustrate the principles discussed in this book.

Pastoral counseling, to me, was a thrilling opportunity to assist people in the application of the principles of the Bible. Some people can accept these principles as preached in the church and make their own application. Others, because of background, temperament, and other factors, need personal help in making these applications. When people go to see a medical doctor or a dentist, they basically seek two things: diagnosis for the cause of their problem and a prescribed cure.

I looked upon people coming to a counselor much in the same manner. They wanted me to diagnose their problems and thought I could do it more objectively because of my training and experience. Since I was not wholly involved with them emotionally, people usually expected me to be objective about who was right or wrong and provide them a remedy based on the Word of God. The secret to this therapy was really in the hands of the patients. If they took their "medicine"—if they accepted the principles of God, thus introducing the power of God into their lives and marriages—then they could expect a cure.

Not all of my counseling efforts were successful. Sometimes people refused to accept the principles of God and incorporate them into their lives. Sometimes people agreed that the principles were right, but they were so stubbornly self-willed that they refused to exchange their habits and way of life for God's ways. A doctor can't do much for an obese patient who refuses to change his or her eating habits. Neither could I do much for selfish, domineering, fearful, or profligate individuals unless they were willing to face their shortcomings in the light of God's Word and then ask God for the power to change their habits and way of life.

Let's take a look at our first case study.

A Twenty-Five-Year Procrastination

After church one night a middle-aged man named Art asked to see me. "I need God," he said. Later Art told me that his father, a minister, had begged him repeatedly to receive Christ, but Art had refused. Now, after twenty-five years of marriage, Art realized he had been selfish, caustic, and cruel to his wife—and he had destroyed his marriage to boot. Nancy had just told him she no longer loved him and wanted a divorce, so he felt that he should come back to God.

I have to say that Art already knew the gospel well when I presented it to him. He received Christ by confessing his sins and inviting Jesus Christ into his life as Lord and Savior. I gave him some Scripture verses that assured him of his salvation and offered a few suggestions on how to read the Bible and pray. As he was leaving, Art asked, "Would you counsel with my wife?"

"Naturally," I said.

When his wife, Nancy, walked into my study a few days later, I was not quite prepared for what I encountered. A sharp-looking owner of a beauty shop, she was every inch a dynamic human being. "I've had it," she said. "Art has cursed me, hit me, belittled me, criticized me, scolded me, and verbally harassed me until I have nothing but hatred in my heart for him. The sooner he gets out of my life, the better off I will be."

Nancy had been planning and saving for years so that when her daughter finished high school, she would be financially independent. She had reached her goal of being "free to come and go as I please." Nancy refused to talk of spiritual things because, she said, "If I accept Christ, I will have to stay with Art the rest of my life, and I'd rather roast in hell first. Besides, I never should have married Art in the first place!"

I realized that this woman of choleric temperament had been miserable for many years. She didn't know it, but worse days were ahead if she persisted in her angry mood of hostility. Ever since their first week of marriage, Nancy's melancholy husband had been a disappointment to her. Although Art loved her, he continually found fault with her because she didn't meet his perfectionist standards. She was incensed at his criticism because he was so moody and indecisive that it took him forever to accomplish anything. Because Nancy was the faster talker, she would lash him with words until Art would become frustrated and strike her.

After he accepted Christ, Art began coming to church regularly and grew spiritually by leaps and bounds. Every time I saw him, however, I couldn't help thinking, *If only he had received Christ as a young man. Then he would have been less selfish and critical and would have foregone all this heartache. He would have been more loving and kind to his wife. His home would not have been destroyed.* So many couples are unaware that angry, cruel words, like deep physical wounds, leave lasting scars.

I still remember my last counseling session with Nancy. "The Lord will be around to help you pick up the pieces of your life if you will just turn to him," I said. She nodded and left, but I don't know whether she ever repented of her self-will or gave God a chance to change her.

The Healing of God

Most of my counseling experiences had happier endings. Once, I counseled a choleric woman and a melancholy man who were almost identical to the couple just mentioned, except they had been married only ten years. After a fling at being a cocktail waitress and doing whatever she wanted with her life, Melanie finally faced the fact that at thirty-four years of age, she was a very miserable woman. Her melancholy husband, Rodney, had grown so much spiritually that she could not help but see the changes in him. Melanie observed her husband exhibiting a new gentleness and thoughtfulness with their children that had been unheard-of before.

Now Rodney was more patient, understanding, and considerate. In fact, he displayed a new air of confidence that made it easier for him to make decisions and be flexible under pressure. Melanie finally realized that Jesus Christ had so corrected her husband's weaknesses that he was superior to any of the other men she knew, so she asked for a reconciliation.

Spiritual Lethargy

Another wife of choleric temperament came to see me one day and tearfully told how she and her husband were slowly drifting apart. Magdalena loved her husband, Alexandro, and she felt he loved her, but she said, "Another six months like this, and we will hate each other."

Magdalena's talented but easygoing husband was in business with his father. She and his father clashed over the way he ran the business. She said, "If he keeps it up the way he is going, we will soon be bankrupt." It seems a Christmas party at the in-laws had erupted into an explosion that almost equaled the blasts at the Nevada nuclear testing grounds.

All the folks involved were professing Christians. As we talked, however, Magdalena admitted her own spiritual lethargy and the awful anger and hostility that she permitted to run rampant in her life. From her point of view, she had human justification to be angry. And, as she let things fester and stew in her mind, calm communication became impossible. Magdalena built up to such a point that she would explode with angry, sarcastic words that caused others unnecessary pain. She really didn't mean them and would like to have taken them back.

We read and talked about Ephesians 4:30-32. Magdalena finally realized that all anger and wrath are sins. With that realization she took the first big step. She then understood that her job was to follow Christ's example and heed his instructions on being a wife and mother—and try not to run her husband's business.

"But isn't there something I can do about the unchristian principles my father-in-law is bringing into our firm? I'm sure if he keeps this up he will destroy it! Do I have to sit back and do nothing?" she asked. They were honest questions.

"There are several things you can do," I replied. "Get right with

God yourself, concentrate on walking with him, and commit the business to him. When the Holy Spirit leads you, you might 'speak the truth in love' to Alexandro. But not in anger! Remember, he is caught in the crossfire of emotional loyalties between his parents and his wife. Your marriage is far more important than the business. It's your job to be a good wife; it's God's job to take care of the business. Concentrate on being a loving, gracious wife—and let God handle the business." I then shared with her how the Holy Spirit could overcome her weakness, and she went home.

Soon Alexandro began to realize that his wife had changed. As she relaxed and quit pressing him, he lost his resentment toward her. The spark returned to their marriage. When Alexandro didn't hear her voice nagging him, he could hear God speak to him about his spiritual indifference. As Alexandro grew spiritually, he became alarmed about his father's business procedure and insisted on changes in various policies. The business began thriving, but more important was the change in this couple's relationship with each other and with God.

Afterward, they sent one of their neighbors whom they had led to Christ to see me. When I asked the woman what had caused her to accept the Savior, she replied, "It was Alexandro's and Magdalena's home life; I never saw anything like it. These people had a love for each other that I had never seen before."

Fears Overcome

The power of Jesus Christ to cure fear is graphically illustrated by the story of the wife of a neurologist. Sandy came to see me at the recommendation of some neighbors. Her lifelong fears had developed into a phobia after her father committed suicide, and they were gradually getting worse. She experienced long periods of depression and became panicky about being alone. She felt an unusual muscular restriction when surrounded by strange people at a mall, for instance. "I became phobic in elevators," she confided. Her fears caused her husband, Richard, to draw away from her. Finally, their marital situation came to a crisis when her doctor-husband lost patience with her and angrily told her, "I have to deal with women like you all day. I don't want to come home to one every night."

Though terribly insecure, Sandy loved her husband dearly. Only God knew whether she would have really followed through on her threats of self-destruction if he had left her. But she is so transformed today it is very doubtful that he would want to. During her first interview with me, she invited Jesus Christ into her life. In subsequent interviews, I pointed out some of the causes of her fears and prescribed God's method of cure.

At first it was hard for her to face the fact that her depression was caused by her thinking pattern of self-pity. When she told her story it wasn't hard to see that as a child she resented her father's drinking and developed the habit of feeling sorry for herself because of the unhappy life she and her mother had lived. I showed her that if she faced her self-pity as a sin, confessed it (1 John 1:9), and asked God to take away the habit of feeling sorry for herself (1 John 5:14-15), then he would.

Then I suggested that Sandy look forward to what lay ahead (Philippians 3:13-14). It took some time, but Sandy gradually learned how to give thanks (1 Thessalonians 5:18) instead of complaining. Depression soon began to lose its tyrannical hold upon her. There were times when she reverted back to her old self-pity and became depressed, but that happened less frequently, and it was not as severe as it once had been.

The fear problem was more complex. Part of it was caused by guilt feelings for the way she felt about her father before his death. This seemed to dissolve as Sandy realized the extent of her forgiveness as revealed in the Bible. Another part was gradually removed by doing a Bible study on fear and peace. As she realized that she had a constant companion who "sticks closer than a brother" (Proverbs 18:24); that Jesus said, "I will never leave you nor forsake you" (Hebrews 13:5, NKJV); and that he promised, "Lo, I am with you always" (Matthew 28:20, NKJV); her lifelong feeling of insecurity was being replaced by faith.

Sandy was fortunate in having a Christian friend who took her regularly to a women's Bible class. The Bible study and Christian friendship were excellent therapy because they helped Sandy face the fact that she had been a very selfish woman. As soon as the Holy Spirit came into her life, Sandy began to show interest in the lives of other people. The more she lost herself in others, the less fearful she became.

It didn't take long for her analytically minded and medically trained husband to recognize that Sandy had changed. He wasn't ready to admit that a personal relationship with Jesus Christ had caused the changes in his wife, but he conceded that something had transformed her.

The power of Christ to overcome fear is not limited to a particular age. One day a woman two years short of retirement came in to say that she had received Christ in one of our women's Bible classes but felt "that it didn't work." Dee had tried several religious and psychological approaches to overcome her fears, but none of them had helped. Dee's fears kept her from sleeping, and insomnia made her nervous and irritable. She had high blood pressure and worried constantly. "The only thing that seems to help me is when I come over here late at night and sit on the front steps of the church and pray," Dee said.

Her father, whom she loved and admired, had been a liberal

minister. He had taught that the Bible is a "good book, but full of myths and legends and should be taken symbolically." Consequently, Dee couldn't understand or benefit from the Word of God because she invariably doubted everything she read. After several interviews in which I gave her a spiritual prescription—reading the Bible for at least ten minutes a day and memorizing one verse of Scripture—Dee's life changed. Then one day she said, "It's no longer necessary for me to have counseling. God has transformed my life."

I could see it in Dee's eyes.

Misplaced Blame

A young businessman named Mike came in one day acknowledging his faults and weaknesses. Then he brought up his real problem: His wife, Gaby, had very low sexual desire. "It wasn't always this way," he said. "We met at a Christian group in college, and we were committed to staying out of bed. But it wasn't long before things went too far and we made love."

Gaby became pregnant during one of their trysts. They decided that they would do the right thing and get married, but neither finished college. They gave up all thoughts of Christian service, and Mike's lack of a college degree limited his ability to find a good-paying job. Mike said that he tried to be thoughtful and kind, but Gaby rapidly lost interest in any physical contact. Knowing there are always two sides to every marital problem, I asked him to have his wife come see me.

When his wife of eleven years came in and tearfully cried, "I hate sex!" I knew she had some deep-rooted problems. Before discussing the physical maladjustment, I asked a few questions about Gaby's children and her marriage in general. I recognized that Gaby was a bundle of nerves, bordering on neurosis because of her intense hostility and bitterness. She was completely frustrated. Every dream in her life had been smashed. She had wanted to be a virgin when she married, she said, but Mike couldn't control his passion. She had wanted to be a music teacher and to see her husband rise up in the corporate ranks, she said, but neither of them qualified for more than hourly-wage jobs.

"Mike is never home," she complained. "He has to work two jobs to pay the bills, and he never does anything around the house. We don't have a decent car, house, or furniture. Nothing I dreamed of has worked out, and it's all his fault!"

I frowned. As for their physical relationship, usually such an emotionally expressive woman has learned, after eleven years of marriage, to enjoy sex thoroughly, particularly when her husband is kind, clean, and considerate.

It took some convincing to help Gaby realize that although her husband had his faults and weaknesses, her attitude was the real problem. She felt excessive guilt for having violated her standards when they had premarital sex, but she blamed only him. When she finally admitted her sin, she could confess it and experience a tremendous sense of relief. Through an examination of Ephesians 4:30-32, she saw her own hostility and enmity of heart as a sin that grieved the Holy Spirit. Gradually, as Gaby learned to face her anger as a sin, God began putting a new love into her heart for her husband. She began to relax and again became the emotionally responsive wife she had been on their honeymoon.

As Mike and Gaby began praying together, God guided them into a long-range educational program that gave them new goals and objectives. The home that once was cold and hateful became a haven. In fact, Mike admits that he used to seek any excuse to avoid spending time at home; now he guards his opportunities to be with his wife and children because of the joy he experiences in being with them.

Spirituality and Sex

It may strike some Christians as strange to hear a minister say that two Spirit-filled partners can experience more physical and emotional pleasure from the act of marriage—lovemaking—than the average couple, but I definitely believe it. It is a well-known fact that relaxation and unselfishness are primary keys to sexual harmony. What power on earth relaxes people and motivates them to goodness, kindness, and self-control like the Holy Spirit does?

I have the impression that many Christians subconsciously think that when a couple experiences the filling of the Holy Spirit, one of the first things they must do is rush out and buy a set of twin beds. This attitude implies that God wants to put a wedge between them. The truth of the matter is, the urge to make love is a gift of God for a couple's supreme emotional and physical pleasure. The more spiritually sensitive an ordinary Christian couple becomes, the more they may desire to enjoy each other physically.

When the Holy Spirit fills a life, he puts a new love for other people into the heart. He makes couples more patient and kind. It naturally follows that a Spirit-filled husband and wife will be more loving and affectionate toward each other. The "little things" that used to create hostility and resentment are gone; consequently, they will have less emotional resistance to sexual advances and will be more likely to respond to one another. In fact, Spirit-filled people will be less inhibited in the intimacies of marriage. Inhibitions tend to stifle sexual pleasure, particularly for women. Thus, a Spirit-filled woman will gradually relax and more easily attain fulfillment in the experience.

As I look back on my counseling years, I remember only one Spirit-filled couple that came to me sexually maladjusted. They were a young husband and wife who didn't know what they were doing. After we talked, I handed them some books to read for "homework." It wasn't long before they solved their sexual problems. In fact, that experience was what motivated me to write my best-selling book on sexual adjustment in marriage—*The Act of Marriage.*

Spiritually sensitive people are directed by the Holy Spirit to find the solutions to their problems. The spiritual characteristic of meekness overcomes the natural characteristic of pride that often keeps couples from admitting they have a problem. When they acknowledge the problem and seek God's help, he directs them to the right answers. Be sure you carefully read Appendix A: "The Spirit-Filled Person." It will enrich all areas of your marriage.

Hate Changes to Love

I remember the time when I saw probably the best illustration ever of the power of Jesus Christ to change two people. A young couple, Shawn and Elisa, had been visiting our church off and on for about three months. One night they called, explaining that they had to see me right away. I don't think I have ever been more conscious of blatant hatred between two people. There were three chairs in my study. When I said, "Won't you be seated?" they wouldn't even plunk down in chairs next to each other; they purposely left the third seat vacant between them. It didn't take long for them to tell their story.

"She won't let me touch her anymore," Shawn blurted out.

When I nodded in Elisa's direction, she said, "My father was an alcoholic. When Shawn and I got married seven years ago, he promised me that he wouldn't drink if I married him. Now he drinks every night on the way home from work. Friday nights are the worst; he comes home drunk. I can't stand to have him touch me when he's been drinking."

"You were that way before I started drinking!" he snapped. As we talked, it became apparent that this couple had two fundamental problems. Sure, Shawn and Elisa had other minor irritants, but basically they were sexually frustrated because of their selfishness, ignorance, and lack of meaningful communication. More important, neither of them knew Jesus Christ as Savior even though they had been attending my church.

I didn't know which problem to tackle first. Then I remembered the sound advice of my high school football coach: "Never take on two men simultaneously; always concentrate on one or the other." But which problem should I tackle first? I prayed about it, and it seemed I should talk with them about their sex life first.

They had married quite young and got along sexually very well following their honeymoon. But as the novelty of marriage wore off, their different backgrounds rose to the surface. She was reared by reserved parents who maintained a quiet household and exhibited etiquette and neatness to others. "I never heard my parents raise their voices at each other, nor have I ever heard my father swear," Elisa stated.

Shawn, reared in a working-class section of the city, had received his sex education in the alley and the Army barracks. Somehow Elisa had never been able to get through to him that the rough language he used to describe various sex acts "turns me off!" She would be aroused, close to orgasm, and all he had to do was innocently say what she considered ugly words and her emotional fire went out. At that point, intercourse became more torture than pleasure.

Each time Shawn wanted to make love, she increasingly

resisted his sexual advances. The more Elisa resisted, the more determined he became. Finally, after being rejected repeatedly, he resorted to drinking just to get back at her.

Shawn's maturity was evident upon his learning that his street language had been a turnoff, not a turn-on, for his wife. Shawn got up out of his chair, took one step closer to Elisa, and said, "Honey, I never dreamed that it was the things I said that offended you. I'm really sorry."

"I can't help it," said Elisa, "but that's the way I feel."

When she burst into tears, he took her hand and earnestly said, "In front of Pastor LaHaye, I want to promise you that you will never hear me say those words again."

Shawn kept his word.

How to Become a Christian

That interchange cleared the sexual chemistry considerably, but I knew that this couple needed an external source of power to help them keep their vows. One evening I asked, "Have you folks ever heard of the *Four Spiritual Laws*?" Finding they had not, I pulled out a little *Four Spiritual Laws* booklet that I always carry in my pocket and said, "Just as God has physical laws that govern his physical universe, so he has spiritual laws that govern his relationship to man." These are the laws I showed Shawn and Elisa that evening:

1. God loves you and has a wonderful plan for your life.

> *For God so loved the world that he gave his only Son, so that everyone who believes in him will not perish but have eternal life.* JOHN 3:16

> *My purpose is to give life in all its fullness.* JOHN 10:10

2. We are sinful and separated from God, thus we cannot know and experience God's love and plan for our lives.

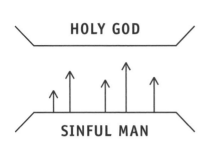

For all have sinned; all fall short of God's glorious standard. ROMANS 3:23

For the wages of sin is death, but the free gift of God is eternal life through Christ Jesus our Lord. ROMANS 6:23

3. Jesus Christ is God's only provision for our sins. Through Christ, we can know God's love and plan for our lives.

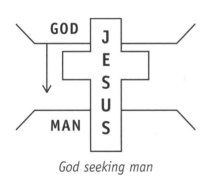

God seeking man

But God showed his great love for us by sending Christ to die for us while we were still sinners. ROMANS 5:8

Jesus told him, "I am the way, the truth, and the life. No one can come to the Father except through me." JOHN 14:6

For God made Christ, who never sinned, to be the offering for our sin, so that we could be made right with God through Christ. 2 CORINTHIANS 5:21

I skimmed through the first three laws, calling attention to the verses and the meaning of each diagram. I knew they already believed the gospel; they just hadn't ever asked Jesus Christ into their lives. Then I said, "This fourth law is the one I want you to look at closely."

4. We must receive Jesus Christ as Savior and Lord by personal invitation.

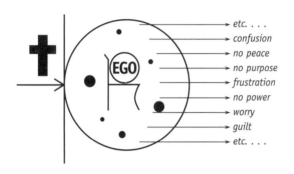

"From this law you can see that it isn't enough to accept Christ as your Savior to forgive your past mistakes," I said. "You also need to accept Christ as your Savior and Lord. You need the Lord to guide your future. This diagram will show you what I mean. The circle represents your lives. The chair represents the control center of your wills. The thing that makes us so different from animals is that God has given us a free will. We can do as we please.

"That is what the word *Ego* on the throne in the circle represents. It is the big 'I.' The dots represent big and little decisions of life that must be made: where I will work, whom I will marry, how I will treat my partner, what kind of friends I will have, and many other decisions. The problem with this life is that Christ is on the outside, and the Ego is making the decisions. As long as we make decisions based on 'What I want,' or 'What is good for me,' we will be filled with degrees of frustration, fear, confusion, purposelessness, guilt, and many other problems.

"Now, if you are willing to receive Christ into your life as Lord and Savior, the result will be different. Christ will come into your life and take over this throne. The first thing Christ does is pardon and cleanse all your sins. That produces peace in your heart, because when your sins are forgiven, you no longer fear God. He

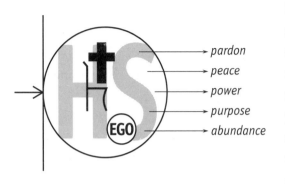

pardon
peace
power
purpose
abundance

becomes a new source of power that enables you to fulfill his thrilling new purpose in your life. Furthermore, Christ, through his Spirit, gives you a new

abundance of life: new love, joy, and peace. These are your basic needs.

"It really isn't hard to receive Christ into your life. John 1:12 says, 'But to all who believed him and accepted him, he gave the right to become children of God.' The Lord Jesus said, 'Behold, I stand at the door and knock. If anyone hears My voice and opens the door, I will come in to him and dine with him, and he with Me' (Revelation 3:20, NKJV). Receiving Christ is simply recognizing that you want him to come into your life to forgive your past and guide your future. By this act you give yourself emotionally, mentally, and physically to Christ.

"Now I want to ask you two something: Which of these circles represents your life right now?" I held the circles up so they could see them clearly.

Within a few seconds they agreed that the first circle represented both of their lives. Then I asked, "Do you know any reason why you couldn't invite Christ into your lives right now?"

"I don't," Shawn spoke up. "That's just what I need."

"Me, too," said Elisa simply.

Right then these two young people prayed their first prayer.

These weren't profound or long prayers; they simply admitted to God that they were sinners and asked the Lord Jesus to come into their lives as Lord and Savior.

In a moment of time, they became children of God, new creatures in Christ. After I gave them a few thoughts about the assurance of salvation and how to grow in their Christian life, Shawn and Elisa left my office, holding hands.

A week later they were back. They gushed that they were amazed at the changes in their marriage.

"What is the biggest change that you have noticed in yourselves?" I asked.

"The quick and complete return of our love for each other," said Elisa, while her husband grinned.

I continued to watch this couple for several months. Whenever I saw the tender and affectionate way they treated each other—after recalling the hatred and bitterness that had existed between them before—I rejoiced again that the gospel of Jesus Christ was still the "power of God at work, saving everyone who believes" (Romans 1:16).

Before you close this book, may I ask you a question? Which of the circles on pages 146–147 represents your life?

If it's the first one, I urge you to let Christ come into your life and introduce you to abundant living. He has the answer to every problem and difficult situation. Let Jesus direct you in being "happy though married."